Teaching of the Great Mountain
Zen Talks by Taizan Maezumi

南無観世音

延命十句観音経　佛

与佛有因　与佛有縁

佛法僧縁　常楽我浄

朝念観世音　暮念観世音

念念従心起　念念不離心

Teaching of the Great Mountain
Zen Talks by Taizan Maezumi

Edited by
Anton Tenkei Coppens

TUTTLE PUBLISHING
BOSTON • RUTLAND, VT • TOKYO

First published in 2001 by Tuttle Publishing, an imprint of Periplus Editions (HK) Ltd, with editorial offices at 153 Milk Street, Boston, Massachusetts 02109.
Copyright © 2000, 2001 by Kanzeon, Inc.

Library of Congress Cataloging-in-Publication Data

Maezumi, Hakuyu Taizan.
    Teaching of the great mountain : Zen talks by Taizan Maezumi / Anton Tenkei Coppens (editor).
    p.cm.
    ISBN 0-8048-3273-0 (pbk.)
    1. Sōtōshū-Doctrines. 2. Spiritual life--Zen Buddhism. I. Coppens, Anton Tenkei.
    II. Title.

BQ9418.7 .M34 2001
294.3'420427--dc21   2001023347

Distributed by

North America
Tuttle Publishing
Distribution Center
Airport Industrial Park
364 Innovation Drive
North Clarendon, VT 05759-9436
Tel: (802) 773-8930
Tel: (800) 526-2778
Fax: (802) 773-6993

Japan
Tuttle Publishing
RK Building, 2nd Floor
2-13-10 Shimo-Meguro, Meguro-Ku
Tokyo 153 0064
Tel: (03) 5437-0171
Fax: (03) 5437-0755

Asia Pacific
Berkeley Books Pte Ltd
130 Joo Seng Road
#06-01/03
Olivine Building
Singapore 368357
Tel: (65) 280-1330
Tel: (65) 280-3320
Fax: (65) 280-6290

1 3 5 7 9 10 8 6 4 2   06 05 04 03 02 01

Printed in the United States of America

CONTENTS

Even though we are all Kanzeon, without exception,

how come we can't eliminate all our fears

pain, suffering, all kinds of frustrations,

anger, dissatisfaction?

How come? How come?

Maezumi Roshi

Maezumi Roshi and Genpo Sensei in England, 1987.

FOREWORD

This book is based on talks given by Maezumi Roshi to Kanzeon Sangha in 1987 and 1992 in England, The Netherlands, and Poland, and in 1994 at Kanzeon Zen Center in Salt Lake City, Utah. Remembering Maezumi Roshi and the many years I spent with him, my fondest memories go back to the days we traveled together throughout Europe, particularly the time we went to Poland by train. I think I have never seen Roshi so relaxed and happy as on this tour. We traveled in a small group that included Tenkei, and as the hours and days went by we grew more and more intimate. It wasn't always easy, as the train was far from luxurious, and the police and border patrol would wake us up in the middle of the night. But in a way, it was all wonderful. Roshi loved visiting the various European countries and meeting all the students there. I remember him relaxing in a tea shop in England after sesshin. It was cold, and one of the photographs shows him in a heavy sweater that Tenkei's mother had made.

Roshi found the European students very open and receptive, and the talks collected in this book are some of the most inspired I ever heard him give. To put his words on paper is not easy, because although Roshi had a great grasp of vocabulary, his English was not always grammatically correct, and he had very much his own way of saying things. With his innovative style of editing, Tenkei Sensei has been successful in keeping the flavor and spirit of Roshi's teisho. Reading through the text, I really feel I am once again in the presence of Maezumi Roshi and hear him speak as if he were alive.

As a successor of Maezumi Roshi, I feel honored to present this book, especially because it is edited by one of my own successors. It brings up something that Roshi often addressed. He always said that he felt like a stepping stone for bringing the dharma to the West. Now, as a link between Roshi and Sensei, I too feel like a stepping stone for the next generation. For Zen to really take root in the West many changes will need to be made, but the essence of the teaching expressed in these talks should not be lost.

As I am writing this preface early in the new millennium, I feel that this book is coming out at a very appropriate time. It is fitting that a broader audience be exposed to Maezumi Roshi's dharma. He had great faith in the strength of a diverse sangha. According to him, sangha may become the most important principle of Buddhism in modern times. I think there is a lot of wisdom in his prediction. As we look into the future, it is going to be crucial that we work together in harmony, not only as a Buddhist family but also as a global community. I hope that the following pages will be a contribution to this harmony.

Dennis Genpo Merzel

EDITOR'S INTRODUCTION

Taizan ("Great Mountain") Maezumi Roshi (1931–1995) was one of the great pioneers of modern Zen. Alongside a handful of other Japanese masters, he turned the wheel of dharma in our age and opened up a unique tradition of Buddhist practice to a worldwide movement. His position was a particularly interesting one. As a successor in three different lineages of the Soto as well as the Rinzai schools, he could draw from an exceptionally rich background and express the teaching of the Buddha in a very broad and colorful way. He guided thousands of students and produced twelve successors, who spread his teaching all over the world. Yet so far, very little of this teaching has appeared in print.

One of the reasons may be that although Maezumi Roshi was a powerful speaker, his propensity to mix scholarly expertise with a direct and often whimsical, if not mischievous, intuition does not make it easy to capture his words alive. Moreover, his free use of language sometimes led to long adventures of digression, weaving a web that connected him with the audience very intimately, but left anyone in the dark who would try to pin him down on anything. His profound understanding of the dharma simply defied definition. But that doesn't mean Roshi's teaching was indirect or vague. Rather, he was unpredictable. And fearless. I remember him as somebody who could be sweet as honey at the beginning of a sentence and razor sharp at the end. Or vice versa, whatever the situation asked for. He could be very subtle, but also quite blunt. On one occasion a student asked him, "What do I do with my attachment?" And Roshi yelled, "Be attached!!" At another time somebody asked, "How do I deal with the teacher?" And he snapped back: "Ignore him!"

The first time I heard Roshi speak in the zendo of the Zen Center of Los Angeles some twenty years ago, I was in a mild state of shock. I had come all the way from Holland to hear something that definitely sounded more important than anything I had ever heard before. But what was it? For the first few months I was happy if I could just determine whether he was speaking Japanese or English. But Roshi always captured my attention completely. And although he was not my direct teacher—I'm a student of his successor, Genpo Merzel Roshi—I've had the great fortune to hear him on many occasions. As time passes, I realize more and more what an indelible impression his talks have left on me. Grieving over his sudden death in 1995 and looking for a way to be close to him, I began to transcribe some of the audio tapes that I treasure as the quintessential Maezumi Roshi.

One of the things that I greatly appreciated in Roshi was his agility of mind, and I have tried to show that quality as much as possible in this publication. Soon after I started the delicate process of editing, I discovered that the rhythm of his spoken word begged for a poetic format. Turning his grammatical idiosyncrasies into proper English prose would have diminished the original impact of his carefree speech. So the layout of the pages is important. Length of lines and paragraphs and the total visual effect of the text on the page have the purpose of clarifying the meaning.

All the talks in this book were given during sesshins of Genpo Roshi's Kanzeon Sangha, and most took place in Europe.

In the text, Maezumi Roshi sometimes refers to "Sensei." This is Genpo before he received Inka and the title "Roshi." Genpo Sensei invited Maezumi Roshi to Europe several times to join his regular sesshin tours. These tours usually consisted of three or four week-long retreats in various European countries. It was Sensei's way of introducing his teacher to the fast-growing international Kanzeon Sangha, which nowadays has its headquarters in Salt Lake City, Utah. Hundreds of students will be forever grateful to him for this. Maezumi Roshi touched their hearts in his unmistakable manner. He was everyone's grandfather and very happy to share his insights without any restraint. Personally, I feel particularly fortunate to have had the opportunity to travel together with Genpo and Maezumi Roshi. It deepened my connection with both of them. Not only on sesshins but also in planes, trains, and automobiles the intimacy of lineage became a living reality.

The first series of talks, under the title "The Echoless Valley"[1] was give during a sesshin in England on three consecutive days, May 20, 21, and 22 in 1987. It was the last stop on a tour that also included sesshins in Holland and Poland. By the time Maezumi Roshi gave these talks, he had built up a great momentum. I had never seen him so free, the expression of his face and tone of his voice shifting and turning every second. It was as if he were liquid. The theme is the *Sutra of the Seven Wise Sisters* as quoted by Dogen Zenji in the *Eihei Koroku*. The sisters saw a corpse at a crematory and one of them raised the question, "Where did that person go?" Hearing this, all of the sisters attained realization. The god Indra was so impressed that he offered to give them whatever they wanted. The sisters told Indra that they were not particularly short of anything, but would really like to have three things, the Rootless Tree, the Land of No Yin and Yang, and an Echoless Valley. After an introduction to koan study, Roshi investigates these three requests as koans, taking one as the focus for each talk. Along the way, he covers many of his favorite topics and introduces us to various Buddhist masters in such an intimate way that it is sometimes hard to know who is talking. The different voices all seem to blend into one.

The talk on "Mu" was given on the next day, May 23. So in a way, the first four chapters in this book belong together. But although Maezumi Roshi continues the flow of the previous talks and elaborates further on the subject matter, "Mu" clearly stands on its own. Many participants in the sesshin were working on this famous koan, and Maezumi Roshi wanted to give them clear direction. Koan study is often misunderstood and seen as a kind of mind game. For Maezumi Roshi, however, koan is our life itself, and clarifying Mu clarifies this very life. The koan gives us a chance to cut off all dualistic thinking and experience our buddha-nature directly. In this talk particularly, it is very interesting to see how he goes beyond any possible sectarianism. Trained in Soto-style shikantaza practice as well as Rinzai-style koan study, he had multiple entries into the heart of Zen and bridged the gap between the different schools. Also, Maezumi Roshi refers now and then to the *jukai* ceremony, because during these sesshin tours quite a number of participants would receive the Buddhist precepts. The talk presented in Chapter Eight is completely devoted to this subject.

"Kanzeon" is a talk given in Holland on September 12, 1992. Maezumi Roshi was extremely fond of this great Bodhisattva and often elaborated on how she saves all beings from samsara. He loved the name that Genpo Roshi had given to his international organization of students, "Kanzeon Sangha," and wanted to clarify for everyone who Kanzeon really is.

"Genjokoan" was given the next day, September 13, at the same location. The title refers to the first fascicle of Dogen Zenji's masterwork, "Shobogenzo." The life and work of this great thirteenth-century Japanese master was an endless source of inspiration for Maezumi Roshi. And it is hard to imagine any presentation of Roshi's teaching without Genjokoan being one of the major principles. He often mentioned that he saw all of Dogen Zenji's writing summarized in Genjokoan. This fascicle epitomizes how to manifest our life as the life of everyone and everything.

"Jijuyu-Zanmai," part of a talk given in Holland on May 6, 1987 is a small but beautiful exposition of self-fulfilling samadhi. Maezumi Roshi doesn't present this joyful state as something that needs to be attained or accomplished, but as the natural condition of our life.

"Master Zuigan," given during the same sesshin in Holland, is about a famous koan of the *Mumonkan* collection. Dharma talks by Zen masters are called *teisho* in Japanese, meaning a direct expression of the dharma. So a teisho is not "about" the dharma, it is a manifestation of the dharma itself. It's great and also endearing to see how Maezumi Roshi completely identifies here with Master Zuigan. As the story goes, Zuigan used to sit zazen on a big rock, calling to himself over and over again, "Hey, boss! Are you in?" On the day he gave this talk, Roshi clearly suffered from jet lag after a long flight from Los Angeles to Amsterdam and couldn't help dozing off now and then. So he called out to wake up himself and everyone else. But he raises an interesting question. What is it that we really have to wake up to? What are most of us unaware of?

"Shikantaza" was given in Poland on May 15, 1987. Maezumi Roshi addresses the practice of "just sitting" as the best way to appreciate our life. He says it is jijuyu-zanmai, self fulfilling samadhi, or just being. That doesn't mean shikantaza stands for something static or dull. Roshi calls the intimacy of it revealing. This may be a good place to emphasize that for him there is no real difference between shikantaza and koan. Although the methods may appear different, intrinsically they are one and the same: the realization of this very life. Roshi often uses the words shikantaza and koan in connection with each other. For example in the talk "Mu" he calls shikantaza the best answer to our seeking mind. And once, during a group discussion, he made up an interesting koan, "What is shikantaza?" No one could present a response that satisfied him.

"The True Dharma Eye" was given on May 13 during the same sesshin in Poland. The order of the chapters in this book obviously doesn't always follow the chronological order of the talks. Since it was my intention to present a kaleidoscopic collection of Maezumi Roshi's teisho rather than a linear structure of his teaching, I have tried to create an organic whole where pieces just seem to fit in place. In the "True Dharma Eye" he elaborates on an interesting implication of "Shobogenzo," the title of Dogen Zenji's masterwork. Shobogenzo is usually translated as "Treasury of the True Dharma Eye." To clarify what this "eye" really is, Maezumi Roshi follows the understanding of Harada Roshi, who was the teacher of one of his own teachers, Yasutani Roshi. The True Eye can be divided into two eyes, one that sees the absolute equality of the world and one that sees the differentiation of all phenomena. If we don't have both eyes, or rather if we are not able to see in both ways, we get into trouble. So the point is to be flexible and not to get stuck anywhere. This exemplifies beautifully one of the essentials of Maezumi Roshi's teaching. Whatever understanding we reach, when we become attached to it, we are bound to create suffering for our self and others.

"Kai" was also given during this Polish sesshin. It discusses the familiar Buddhist precepts, but from a very mature perspective. Using the poems of Bodhidharma and Dogen Zenji on several precepts, Maezumi Roshi goes far beyond conventional interpretations.

The chapter "God" is from a talk given at Kanzeon Zen Center in Salt Lake City, Utah on April 15, 1994. Roshi visited the Center for the inauguration of the new zendo. He had brought as a gift a statue of Manjusri that would replace the figurine of Kanzeon on the altar. Maezumi Roshi compares the different functions of these bodhisattvas and then moves on to questions concerning God. Students wondered how to respond to members of the LDS (Mormon) church when asked whether or not they believed in God. The discussion took a hilarious turn when a student said, "I would answer, 'I am God, who are you?' But I'm afraid I would offend." Roshi smiled and said very sweetly, "Yes, because it's not true!!"

"Ceremony" was also given in Salt Lake City. Maezumi Roshi often worked on this topic, particularly in the last years of his life. Here he shows that the formal dress code, etiquette, and services in Zen do not only express respect for tradition. They also have a healing function.

"The Four Dharma Seals" was given two years earlier, in September 1992 in Poland, but seemed a good subject to conclude this collection of talks. It is a beautiful example of Maezumi Roshi's ingenuity and subtlety. The Four Seals are basic standards set up to determine whether or not a teaching can be considered Buddhist. Traditional Buddhism often mentions only three seals:

impermanence, no-self and suffering. Maezumi Roshi goes beyond the one-sided view that the traditional interpretation of the seals can lead to. Using a line from the Enmei Jukku Kannon Gyo (a short chant dedicated to Kanzeon), *Jo Raku Ga Jo,* he provides a refreshing look into these seals and flips their meaning completely. They become permanence, joy, self, and purity,[2] and constitute the characteristics of our life as seen through the eyes of Kanzeon Bodhisattva. What better encouragement could Roshi give for us to realize who we really are. In the last paragraph, he almost begs us, "Please go back to do good zazen."

Maezumi Roshi's teaching has always struck me as being a very intimate one. He opened people's hearts by exposing his own. I hope some of that quality will shine through the pages of this book and reach a larger audience. For me, putting Roshi's words on paper has brought me closer to him than ever before, and I wish I could thank him for that. But then again, I think I know what he would tell me. Students often openly expressed their gratitude after listening to a teisho. In response, he sometimes just giggled and said, "But I am benefitting the most!" This time, however, I would challenge that. Delving into his teaching, I feel that I am the one who benefits the most. I wish every reader the same.

Anton Tenkei Coppens
Salt Lake City, Utah

[1] These three talks were originally published as a minibook, *The Echoless Valley*, edited by Anton T. Coppens. Mt. Tremper, NY: Dharma Communications, 1998.

[2] It is interesting to note that in *The Awakening of Faith,* by Asvaghosha, these characteristics are called the Attributes of Suchness (pp. 65–67, by Y. S. Hakeda, Trans., 1967, New York: Columbia University Press).

Part One
THE ECHOLESS VALLEY

The Rootless Tree

So many things to be said about koan.
Even to define what koan is varies.
Easily you can find half a dozen
different definitions of what koan is.
On top of that, how each understands koans.
So even by these two major reasons, see
the implication of koan,
how ambiguous it might become.
Even if I ask you, maybe all of you
might answer in a slightly different way.
So this koan, even though
it sounds paradoxical
and might not make much sense,
it is very important.
Myself I learned, studying koan,
even though it was in a rather poor way that I pursued it.
I learned a lot.
So it's fine. I want all of you to learn
something from koan study, by koan study.
We shouldn't get mixed up about koan studies.

We don't study koans.
In a way we do and in a way we don't.
We do it if we take koan as life itself.
Living itself. Yes.
Studying koans is not the way to do it.
If koan is something apart from your life.
That's what happens, see, as
shortcomings of koans, koan studies.
What we study is, as Dogen Zenji said, about oneself.
Not only Dogen Zenji. Great Rinzai masters all say that.
Second Patriarch of Japanese Rinzai lineage, Daito Kokushi,
he says that to study oneself, not just study, see,
penetrate and really see.
Realize what self is.
Not only realizing, actualizing.
In a way, it's the same thing.
Without actualization
one can't be really understood.
So how we really study the self?
In order to study the self
we use koans.

That's one way to look at it, see.
So koan study shouldn't be the main thing.
The main thing is always oneself.
And when oneself and the koan become identical
that's the moment of realization
of koan, *genjokoan*.
That's what Dogen Zenji talks about—
to pursue such life as everyday life.

In four talks, I try to deal with not only what
is the koan and how we appreciate koan
or how Dogen Zenji talks about koan
but how the koan could be appreciated
in a different way.
The koans we use, the so-called
kosoku koans, which are already sort of
originated by someone else and put in a certain order
to go through. Dogen Zenji talks about koans
a little bit differently, see.
Actually that was his objection when he went to China.
The koan practice which was studied in China at that time
in the Sung Dynasty, he didn't think that was the proper way,
the adequate way to practice koans,
which I agree with perfectly.
He himself studied koans.
Then after he came back from China,
he started to present his way of how to appreciate koan.
That's actually what Shobogenzo is.
His most exquisite writings,
known as *Kaji Shobogenzo*, distinguishing
one more kind of Shobogenzo, which is a koan collection.

But, the koan that I am thinking of sharing with you
for this sesshin, is not from this koan collection of Dogen Zenji
which is called the *Shinji Shobogenzo*, the Chinese Shobogenzo,
but from *Eihei Koroku*, another of his writings in Chinese.
In the first volume this koan is found.
Actually he makes up koan.

That's what I want to share with you,
dividing that one koan in three parts.
In the *Eihei Koroku*, Dogen Zenji quotes from the Sutra,
then makes a koan out of it.
And he gives commentaries to it.
And these commentaries are to be understood as koans,
not understood, be appreciated as a koan.
So he talks about three koans,
giving two commentaries to each of them.
So it becomes six koans in this one case.
I may bring a few other koans in, so we appreciate
at least a dozen of koans together for this sesshin.

In the Sutra, it says something like this.
In India, this supposedly happened about the time of Buddha.
When you really become particular about it scholastically,
when it was really written, it becomes ambiguous.
At the time of the Buddha no Sutra was written.
Later on it was added.
We don't know how true it is, but anyway
it's recorded as the *Sutra of The Seven Wise Women*.

These seven wise ladies in India were of a noble family,
aristocrats, maybe of Brahman class,
rich and well established.
They didn't do much; everything was taken care of
by someone else in one way or another.
Practically all they did was just amuse themselves.
It was custom, just like these days, every weekend
to go someplace else or have a party of some sort,
enjoy themselves.

Then, one of these days,
one of these seven wise ladies told the others
— they could be sisters,
but not necessarily blood sisters —
"Today, instead of going to parties,
let's go to the crematory.
I have a feeling that something nice will happen."
Some people have a sort of supernatural power,
extrasensory sort of awareness; I believe that.
Shakyamuni himself said
he had these five so-called occult powers.
He was even called a magician,
as well as great medical doctor, medicine-king.
So it's quite obvious
that he could perform certain miracles.

Anyway, the seven of them go to the crematory.
And they see a corpse.
And that one lady asked the six sisters,
"A dead corpse is here;
where did the man go?"

We have a very similar koan
Three Barriers of Master Tosotsu
about death.
How to be free from life and death
and if you know how to be free
also you should know where to go.
Where do you go?
Anyway, dead corpse is here;
where the man left for?

By hearing that word, it is said that
all of them attained realization together.
The story goes on, but I want you to think about
what kind of realization they reached.

The story goes that Indra
was watching from heaven,
and he was very pleased.
It says that he made rain of flower petals
with fragrance, celebrated them.
He descends to them and asks them,
"You are marvelous!
I would like to give you something in reward.
What do you want?"

These ladies were born in rich families
born in a very high class.
So they told Indra,
"Practically we have everything.
As far as our life goes,
everything is nicely provided.
We have enough jewels.
We don't particularly want anything.
But if you really want to give us something
we should like to have three things
if you can give them to us."
And Indra said, "Sure, say it."
Then they said, "First, please give us
the rootless tree.
And second, please give us
the piece of land where is no yin and yang.

No day, no night
no woman, no man
no pair of opposites.
That's the land we should like to have.
And third we should like to have
an echoless valley.
These three we should like to have."
Then Indra says, "I can't do it,
and even shravaka and pratyekabuddhas,
the Enlightened Ones, Arhats,
the ideal figures of Theravadan tradition
can't do that.
Only great Bodhisattvas know what they are,
and only the Buddha knows how to get them.
So why don't we go to the Buddha
and ask him."

Dogen Zenji there interrupts that story
and he brings up a koan.
Since Indra didn't answer, I will speak
taking the place of Indra.
What is that Rootless Tree?
Dogen Zenji says,
"The Cypress Tree in the Garden
that's what it is."
Some of you, I'm sure
must have heard about this koan
Joshu's Cypress Tree.
Anyway that's Dogen's first answer.
The Rootless Tree is the Cypress Tree in the Garden.
And he said, "If you don't understand

I pick up my staff and say—
This is It.
The alive Rootless Tree."
What does this Rootless Tree stand for?
We can say all kinds of things, such as
freedom, liberation,
even we can say it's nirvana
not sticking any place.
Easy to say, but how hard it is
the Cypress Tree in the Garden.

A monk asks Joshu,
"What is the most important thing in Buddha's teaching,
what is the primary teaching of the Awakened?"
He answers, "That's what it is,
The Cypress Tree in the Garden."
And the monk asks further,
"No, don't answer me
with that sort of dichotomy
subject-object relationship.
Don't show me dealing with the object."
The monk looks at trees in the yard as objects.
That's all we do.
Then Joshu said,
"I am not showing you dealing with the object."
Then the monk asks the same question,
"What is the primary principle of the Buddhas?"
And Joshu says,
"The Cypress Tree in the Garden."
And Dogen Zenji said,
"That's the Rootless Tree."

When we look into ourselves,
how much my ego sticks up.
Hard question.
It's the same thing when we
penetrate into what Buddha said
when he attained realization.
Some people say this is a Mahayana text,
it is not even Buddha's teaching.
Of course we don't think so in these days,
but sometimes some people
thought that kind of thing
because it is all a little later
and added on top of these very early writings.
So it is hard to say
how much really is the Buddha's teaching.
We take it all as Buddha's teaching.
That is our tradition.

In the *Denkoroku*, the *Transmission of the Light*,
it is said that Shakyamuni Buddha,
looking at the star Venus,
realized the Way and said,
"I and all beings, the great earth,
have simultaneously attained realization."
How do you take that koan?
It is exactly the same
what the Buddha is talking about
and what Joshu is talking about
and Dogen Zenji is talking about.
Exactly they're talking about the same thing.

What are they talking about?
Of course they're talking about the Rootless Tree.
What is that Rootless Tree?
What is that koan?
What's that?
If you don't know,
I raise up this staff and say,
"That is it!"

That one, this one,
what's all this business anyway?
Me, you,
mine, someone else's.
What is that?
This is it!
What is Dogen Zenji talking about—
same thing or different thing?
If you say same thing
you fail.
If you say different thing
also you fail.
How do you take care
of these two different expressions?
"Cypress Tree in the Garden"
and
"This is it!"
Either way you say it
it fails.
Then what are you going to do?
With your own words
what would you say?

If someone asks me, I say
"Rootless Tree has wonderful roots,"
as simple as that.
Not such a good answer
that's for sure.
Anyway, where is that root?
How far down is it firmly rooted?
All these testing points of koan
are part of koan practice.
It is a wonderful practice,
koan.
What is the most basic thing about koan?
It doesn't matter how we put it
—koan, you, your life—
in a way it's the same.
What is the most important thing
about your life?
Obvious
your life,
isn't it?
Then what is it?
What is it?

That's what the koan is.
That's all they are talking about,
and Dogen Zenji, he objects to koan practice,
yet he himself
always talks about koan.
His writing,
it's all koans.

He appreciates koans
as genjokoan,
that is to say, as his life.
That is what genjokoan is,
and that's what you are doing,
at least that's what you want to do.
Actually you are doing it.
What is this life?
Who am I?
What am I?

That's exactly what the Sixth Patriarch asks Ejo.
He had two successors,
and because of these wonderful two successors
we have this wonderful teaching
these days
still
thousands of years later.
Who are you?
How come you are there?
That is the question.
What is there?
Where did you come from
standing there?
If I present anything in particular
as the answer,
it is not It.

The Sixth Patriarch asks further.
Does it have anything to do with practice-realization?
There is a practice.

Sure, there is a realization
enlightenment
in all different degrees,
but one way or another
it can't be defiled.
How we practice
in one way or another
solid massive defilement.

Anyway, this is the koan.
Always, this is the koan.
What is this?
And Dogen Zenji answers
"This is it!"
What kind of this is that?
That's what the Rootless Tree is.
The Cypress Tree in the Garden.

Traditionally, the important point in our practice
is to see this Rootless,
see this less
lessness.
That's what we call emptiness,
shunyata.
That's what Dogen Zenji says
at the beginning of *Shobogenzo, Genjokoan,*
realization of koan.
"All the dharmas are without self."
That's the way it exists.
In other words, all dharmas are nothing but
Rootless.

All dharmas are selfless.
That selfless is the key to understand this Rootless Tree.
Carrying big ego, what can you do?
Dharma can't be defiled, that's for sure
even if we do stupid things;
that's for sure, we do stupid things.
Dharma can't be defiled.
Dharma is indestructible to begin with.
We destruct ourselves.

The Sixth Patriarch's koan is a wonderful koan;
how Nangaku responds, a marvelous koan.
It's all about this Rootless Tree,
Rootless life,
your life,
which exists right now as is.
How do you take it?
That's our first koan.

Maezumi Roshi on the train to Poland, 1987.

The Land of No Yin and Yang

Next koan is
the piece of land where there is no yin and yang,
the land that has no pair of opposites,
no dualism, no dichotomy.
What kind of land could that be?
Dogen Zenji says, taking the place of Indra,
I respond to that, see,
and he said first,
"the crematory,
that's where it is."

All these seven wise ladies
being led by one of them
"Instead of going to parties
let's go the crematory.
Something nice might happen there."
Then they went to that crematory.
That's Dogen Zenji's answer, see,
the land where is no yin and yang,
it's a crematory!
How do you understand that?
Isn't it a nice koan?

What does that crematory stand for?
If you don't understand,
if you can't handle it, I would say,
"The world in the ten directions,
that's what it is,"
that's what Dogen Zenji said.
What is the relationship between
the crematory, the place where corpses are burned,
and all the ten directions
everywhere?

Isn't it a marvelous koan?
He is not talking about something
that makes you purposely puzzled.
I don't think so.
He is quite serious, see.
This pair of opposites,
always that's somehow what gives us a problem.
Of course they're talking about death here
see, life and death
coming and going, existing, not existing
realization, no realization
enlightenment, delusion
whatever.
Good bad, right wrong, this or that
everything somehow goes in pairs.

This man is dead,
where he did he go?

Same thing could be said
we are alive.
Where are we?
And what are we doing?
What is life?
That's the question;
that's the answer too.
Crematory, that's what it is.
Crematory as such is the most undesirable place
where we can live or we can go,
we can visit, we can be.
Maybe one of the most gloomy places,
don't you think?
That's what is.
What's that?
That's your koan!

Dogen Zenji said, "To clarify life and death
is the most important matter in life.
Since there is Buddha, all Buddhas
in the midst of life, there is no life, no death.
Then what's there?
If no life, no death,
what's there?"
What is there, is the life of the Buddha.
He continues, "Consider that life and death
is nothing but nirvana.
There is nothing to avoid, dislike as life and death
or just like, hang on to enlightenment, nirvana itself.
Consider that life and death itself is nothing but nirvana,

and doing so, there is a way to transcend life and death."
Isn't that a very clear statement?
Life and death as nirvana
don't be picky
don't choose this or that.
However comfortable your life is
right now at this moment,
I know some of you have pain.
Whatever painful situation you are involved in
consider that as the very life of the Buddha,
the very state of nirvana itself
and be it.

Just live that life.
It doesn't matter whether it is life or hell,
life of the hungry ghost,
life of the animal,
it's okay;
just live that life, see.
And as a matter of fact
no other way.
Where you stand, where you are,
that's what your life is right there,
regardless of how painful it is
or how enjoyable it is.
That's what it is.

That condition never continues forever.
You can even say it changes completely
in less than a second.

This life, death.
I really believe that
when you really see what your life is,
you understand what death is.
Actually that is Buddha's teaching.
He said, "Since there is the Buddha
in the midst of life and death
there is no life and death."

Dogen Zenji quotes the Chinese master Josan—
Kassan or Josan, one or the other.
"If there is no Buddha in life and death
don't be deluded by life and death."
How do you see that?
One says, "If there is Buddha in life and death
there is no life and death,"
and another one says, "If there is no Buddha in life and death,
don't be deluded by life and death."
How do you understand that?

It's a nice koan, eh?
When there is the Buddha in life and death,
there is no life and death
but the life of the Buddha.
When there is no Buddha in life and death,
you are not deluded by life and death.
But for sure that you live your life
as the life of the Buddhas,
Buddha's life as your life.
Also this is our freedom,

our life as the life of the Buddha
as well as Buddhas' lives
as our lives.
What's the difference?
Sure, if we say difference
yes, there is a difference.
If we say same
sure, that's the same.
Have that freedom—
don't stick to any side.

That's what Dogen Zenji is talking about.
Wherever you stand
whatever your life is,
that's what it is.
How can you compare?
Whether it is good or bad, right or wrong,
just that's it, see.
To compare is the worst thing you can do.
What do you compare your life to?
Better or worse
what is the standard?
What is the standard for better or worse?

Crematory, that's what it is.
The life that you have
that's what it is,
isn't it obvious?

Then Dogen Zenji says,
"If you can't handle it,

if you can't really realize your life in such a way,
I will say it one more time—
the whole world in the ten directions
that's what it is."

If you really understand yourself,
everything else
nothing but your life.
That's where the place of no yin and yang is.
When I read this translation of *Genjokoan*
it is very poor still.
See, Dogen Zenji says here,
"If one examines the ten thousand dharmas
with a deluded body and mind
one will suppose that one's mind and nature are permanent.
But if one practices intimately and returns to the true self
it will be clear that the ten thousand dharmas are without self."
Always somehow this is the key.
We are so much caught up by the self, see.
Always I, mine, me.
I have a problem
I have a pain
I have a friction
I am unhappy.
Return to the true self intimately and see
ten thousand dharmas are without self.
Then what happens?
Ten thousand dharmas become your life
and that's what true self is.
Gensha says,
"The world in the ten directions—

nothing but one bright jewel."
Chosa says, "Ten thousand dharmas—
the world in the ten directions
is nothing but the true body.
The true human body,
that's what all ten directions are."
What kind of awareness is that?

Gensha's ten directions are nothing but
one bright jewel.
When you really see your life
with that wisdom
everything is nothing but your life.

For *jukai* one receives the *ketchimyaku*,
the blood lineage.
At the very top is one circle.
That one circle, that's what true life is
and from that one circle Shakyamuni Buddha comes out.
Then after him all these patriarchs in line
and up to me, to Sensei
and from Sensei to you.
After you that line goes up again
and gets into that circle.

Then from your true life
Shakyamuni Buddha comes out.
That's what blood lineage is, see.
You understand that the ten thousand dharmas are without self.
In other words your life turns out to be
everything.

That's what Gensha says,
"The whole world in the ten directions—
just one bright jewel."
This bright doesn't necessarily mean
shiny, sparkling thing.
That crematory, that's what it is;
your life as you are, that's what it is.

Gensha, I like Gensha.
Dogen Zenji liked him very much too;
he went to the monastery of Seppo
and studied only two years.
I wish some of you had that kind of clear turnover.
Sensei is nice
he is so anxious to really deal with you.
Really try hard!
Until thirty Gensha was a fisherman
he was fishing with his father to support himself.
And one day he came to doubt and question.
What am I doing here
fishing?

I don't know if he was very conscious
about killing the fish as such
maybe not,
but maybe he just questioned:
What am I doing here?

I am sure many of you might feel
in the same way too.

Having your career,
doing something else—
are you really satisfied with it?
From time to time you might wonder
what am I doing?
Am I really doing this right,
something that is worthwhile to do?
Actually that's what Gensha maybe felt.
There is a kind of nice story involved in that
but I skip that part.

Suddenly he decided to go to the monastery.
It was lucky he had a wonderful master
in the nearby monastery; it was Seppo's monastery.
And he went there and he studied two years there.
I don't know what he did.
Not much!
What could he do?
Seppo's monastery was very popular, see
according to another koan in the *Blue Cliff Record*.

Later on when Seppo was getting old
there were 1500 monks.
Being one of these hundreds of monks
what can you do?
So two years he was there;
then he decided to go some place else.
Maybe he was thinking
"There are too many monks staying here.
Maybe it's not so great.
Better go and study somewhere else."

Anyway, he leaves and on the way
he runs into a sharp rock and hurts his toe.
What happens?
This body and mind
body, made of four elements
which are empty,
and if it's empty
where does this pain come from?
Those who will attain in such a clear way
are a little different.
If we bang into something,
"Ouch!" that's all
or maybe we just complain
"Who put this here!"
Banging into stone,
"God damn dumb rock!!!"
Isn't it?
His reflection is something different, see.
Where does that pain come from?
Having body
empty
having nothing
where does that pain come from?
Being nothing
how come it's so painful?
Then he attained realization.
Isn't it marvelous?

To explain it is easy.
You figure it out, see.

Same thing what Dogen Zenji talks about
"Crematory, that's what it is."
Principle exactly the same.
"Where does this pain come from?"
He realized.
Then he goes back
and Seppo sees him—
maybe Gensha was different
from most of the monks.
Seppo notices right away
when he comes back and asks
"Hey you, what happened?
You have just left.
Why don't you go for pilgrimage?"
Then Gensha answers to that,
that's what I love,
"Bodhidharma has never ever come from the East.
The Second Patriarch has never gone to the West."

Yesterday I talked about the koan
The Cypress Tree in the Garden.
That's what it is.
A monk asks
"Why did Bodhidharma come from the East?"
Why did he come?
Why is Bodhidharma so significant?
Then Gensha said
"He has never come."
What is that, what is he saying?
Of course, the Second Patriarch didn't go to India,

he has never gone to the West.
That's understandable.
But do you really understand
he has never gone to India?
Where is he then?

You can see that Gensha
Bodhidharma, Second Patriarch
not only one or two of them—
everything, everybody
being with him.
He is the East West South North,
literally ten directions.
Where to go?
And that's the true pilgrimage.
Seppo loved that expression
and he approved Gensha.
Isn't it nice?

That's what he said
—all directions, everything
nothing but one bright jewel—
that's what crematory is
that's what your life is.
The whole world in the ten directions—
that's what it is
that's what Dogen Zenji says.
How would you say it?
That's the second koan.
Give us the piece of land where is no yin and yang,

good bad, right wrong
happy unhappy, enlightened deluded
Buddhas, creatures
life and death.

Since I mentioned jukai and the ketchimyaku
let me say a little more about it.
I like this passage too
where Dogen Zenji says,
"All the Buddhas in the past, present and future
will become Shakyamuni Buddha
at their attainment of buddhahood."
In other words, when you really
realize your true self
you will understand who Shakyamuni Buddha is.
And then he says
"Shakyamuni Buddha is—
this very mind is the Buddha."
One of you came to dokusan and quoted this koan.
This is Baso's famous koan, see
—This very mind is the Buddha—
and Dogen Zenji continues
"What is meant by
This very mind is the Buddha?
Who is that?" he said.
"Penetrate thoroughly with great care."
Those are his words.

He says that you should carefully study this koan
and realize who you are,

realize your life as
this very Mind is the Buddha.
And to really receive
that life of Shakyamuni Buddha,
that's what to receive jukai means.

The Echoless Valley

The third koan:
Calling and no echoing.
The valley which has no echo
for calling, response.
Still I don't know what would be the best translation,
Un-echoing valley
No echoing valley
Echoless valley
Non-echoing valley.
According to these translations
the new ones seem to be slightly different.
Not just un-echoing—
calling and no response.
I shouldn't say "no response"
as you see the best way to respond
is echoless.

We make too much fuss, too much noise,
that's our problem, see.
Anyway that's the third one—
Un-echoing valley,
that's what we want.

And Dogen Zenji says—
What I'll do is this,
having these seven wise ladies
I'll call upon them
"Sisters!"
And if they respond
I will say right there
"I have just given you an echoless valley."
Isn't that nice?
And he says further—
If they don't answer,
don't respond,
I would say
"Indeed
it is un-echoing valley."
Isn't it marvelous?

There is tremendous reality here;
among these three, definitely
this koan is the best.
Non-echoing or
Echoless or
No echoing
it doesn't matter.
No echo.

The point is that you get that spirit
however it is described
however it is explained
however it is expressed.

If you don't get it
it's of no use, see.

I have been with Sensei these past three weeks
mentioning a number of times
state of being Soto—
unknowable ungraspable.
Actually that's what it is.
That is very symbolic, see
my relating to Dogen Zenji,
definitely Dogen Zenji and also that Sutra
which describes what really our life is
and what is the most important thing in life.

It is not expensive jewels, treasures.
What is to be the real treasure?
That's no other than your life,
not only your life
but the life of anything and everything
how it is really existing.
In a way that is our problem,
maybe we know too much
and we know too little.
Actually we don't know anything
and yet we don't admit that fact.
We overestimate our capacity
our intelligence, our knowledge,
so bound to be unhappy.

It is really an amazing thing, see
in one way or another we are all guaranteed

almost like prophecy
that we are all going to become Buddhas.
That's what the Buddha said;
that's what is said in the *Lotus Sutra*
we are guaranteed.
Not only Buddha, that's what all patriarchs say—
all sentient beings are the Buddha.
So what does that mean?

It's interesting, eh? I am not just playing with words.
Buddha is the one who knows nothing
and we are the ones who know something
and because of that we have trouble.
Sure, it is true.
Another thing Sensei talked about
some of you traveling together
in intimacy.
Intimate, I really like that word.

Just yesterday Sensei mentioned
"Roshi, how do you think about Kodo Sawaki Roshi?"
Kodo Sawaki is the teacher of Deshimaru Roshi.
He is a great teacher
and one of his expressions
which he not necessarily originated
"Zazen is to become really intimate with oneself."
That's one way to say it—
to become really intimate.
I don't know what kind of connotation
you give to the word such as intimate,
maybe two persons being together, close;

two persons, that's what we are almost like,
another person living within me.
True self, what's that?
Isn't it that what you believe?
Original face—
what is opposed to original face
artificial face?
I really ask you seriously:
true self, what is opposed to true self?

Again this relates to the things that we talked about before.
Where is no yin and yang
no division, no true and false.
If it is true self
what is the other self?
Is it false self?
You see how not only misleading
how wrong it is to say there is a true self as such
with you within your life.
How can you say that kind of thing?
Of course that's not what you say.
Someone said it. Who said that, do you know?
True self, in fact we say that.
What's that, isn't it hideous?
True self then false self.
What is false self then?
Who are you?
How do you answer?
Is there any difference between you
answering or not answering?
Is there any difference?

Isn't it marvelous?
That's what Dogen Zenji is talking about.
If you respond, right there
I have just given you that echoless valley.
If you don't respond
indeed, that's what it is.
That's what he is saying—
knowing not knowing.

That reminds me of that famous koan
about Master Hogen
who became later the founder of the Hogen school.
Still he was not quite certain, and doing pilgrimage
and he ends up to be at the temple of Master Jizo Keijin.
It was not quite a monastery
maybe just a few people living there
maybe even no monks other than him.

He stayed a few days
and he is just about ready to leave;
then Master Jizo asks Master Hogen
"What is the point of being on pilgrimage?"
How about you
coming here to have sesshin?
Some of you practically going with Sensei
almost wherever he has sesshin
Amsterdam, Poland, England, Maine.
What's that?
Going around, what are you doing?
And Hogen said,

"I just do pilgrimage aimlessly."
How you can say that?
How can you say I'm just doing it
aimlessly? That's nice, eh?
When we reflect upon ourselves,
how do we do?
We are almost worse than beggars
not aimless at all
so many aims
so many goals
so many wants.
If you don't know which one to take
do you really know what you want?

Dogen Zenji said same thing
"Forget the self
when you sit, just sit.
Don't let the mind be busy,
think no thinking.
Don't even expect to become enlightened
or to become Buddha, to be the Buddha"
he said clearly in the instruction for zazen.
Anyway, Hogen said, "I do pilgrimage aimlessly."
When you really do that
there is the freedom, the liberation
and responding to that Jizo said
"Not knowing is most intimate."
With that word Hogen comes to realization.
Then he stays there with Jizo
and succeeds Jizo's Dharma.

Jizo is a successor of Gensha
whom I talked about yesterday.
Gensha is a successor of Seppo
Seppo is the successor of Tokusan
Tokusan is the successor of Ryutan Soshin
Ryutan Soshin is the successor of Tenno Dogo
Tenno Dogo is the successor of Sekito Kisen
then Seigen Gyoshin, then Sixth Patriarch.
This clear cut lineage.

Anyway, it's not knowing
not knowing is most intimate.
"If the sisters don't respond
I would say—Indeed
that's the echoless valley."
Everything is right there.
That's this koan, see.
As I talked about
these case koans, Dogen Zenji,
he practically makes up all these koans
picking up the story from the Sutra.

In fact with Sensei that's what I have been talking about.
In this country, in Europe, in the States
the same koans got to be well utilized—
not even to say utilized,
it's the wrong way to say.
Life is nothing but koan.
That's what Dogen Zenji talks about
as genjokoan.

All life all together
is nothing but koan.
How to really appreciate it, see?

Read the Bible
doesn't matter New Testament, Old Testament
or even the Torah.
Maybe more fascinating
boundless wisdom is there.
You having Jewish background,
how much do you know about your own tradition?
Or being Christian, the same.
You have abundant wisdom there.
How to take it as your life
as your genjokoan?
You have all kinds of wonderful
poetry, drama, literature
that's wisdom.
Look at Shakespeare.
I don't see anyone
who is more enlightened than he is.
Sure, don't you agree with me?
Look how he writes!
He can write any kind of person
from the excellent king to the peasant or the servant
— I don't mean to discriminate upon that —
how he writes practically any characters
more than genius, maybe he is a god.
Even he creates God;
maybe he describes God better

than the God described in the Bible.
I shouldn't say that, I shouldn't go too far.
Anyway you know what I mean.
Maybe you don't!
I don't either!!!

It's marvelous, see.
He really knows how to forget himself
and forgetting himself he could be any character
in any drama.
That's how I understand the way he writes;
it's so marvelous,
a person like him, a genius of the geniuses.
Anyway, not knowing—
by doing so he is most well-functioning
not only as a writer
even as a human being, really marvelous.
I don't know about human being, but at least as a writer.
It gives a kind of idea what Dogen Zenji
is really talking about.
We can say all sorts of things, see.
When you really penetrate in something else,
definitely you are forgetting about everything
but the one thing that you are doing,
and in such a way you are doing the best.

So Genjokoan, let me read
something Dogen Zenji had said.
I thought it kind of quite well fitting
what we are talking about.

"Thus, if one practices and realizes the Buddha Way,
when one gains one dharma
one completes one dharma.
When one encounters one action
one practices one action.
Since the place is here
and the way everywhere
there isn't a limit of the knowable.
Unknowable is simply that our knowledge
arises with and practices with
the absolute perfection of the Buddhadharma.
Do not practice thinking that the realization
must become the object of one's knowledge and vision
and be grasped conceptually.
Even though the attainment is simultaneously manifest,
it's intimate nature is not necessarily realized.
Some may realize it
and some may not."

It's kind of nice and interesting passage
this first part is also very important.
When you meet one dharma, you practice one dharma
when you practice one dharma, you gain one dharma.
In a way it's always one thing at the time.
That's what previous koans are,
even life and death.
When we are alive
definitely we are alive, not dead
so be alive and forget about death.
When we are dead we are not alive,

so don't worry about it.
Isn't it funny?
That's what you do, eh
that's what we all do—
being alive what we all worry about is death.
Isn't it true?
"I'm afraid!"
Afraid of what?
"I don't know."
That's what you say.
Isn't it crazy?

So why don't you live
with your whole heart?
Regardless if you do it or not—
no other way, that's what you are doing.
Being stingy or wholehearted
that's what you got to do.
So just do it, see.
Just do it!
Actually that's what yesterday's part was
no yin and yang.
When you really do it your life manifests as a complete thing;
sometimes we talk about death, dying
and you do it.

I remember Sensei talked about great death.
Sure, when you really do that it works.
It's actually what Dogen Zenji said:
Forget the self.
Drop out body and mind;

another way to say
die, kill yourself,
forget yourself.
For what?

To experience the state of no self—
when you really do that, then what happens
all ten directions become one.
Needless to say, that's the formula.
It doesn't work like the formula says
simply because you are not really doing
according to what formula says.
If you really do,
sure it works.
And there are different kinds of formulas, see
you can't mix up everything.
That's why better have good teacher.
It really works.
It's so important, see, when you do it
just do it, without expectation.
You don't need to expect—
when you do it, it just happens.
But when you expect something, when you aim at something,
right there you dilute your energy;
you split your energy, you split your attention
and it becomes more than the place of yin and yang.
You don't only divide
but you create the problem.

So how can we do that?
It's all together a koan, isn't it?

And when you really grasp the spirit of koan
you can appreciate your life
all together nothing but the koan.
And when you really understand it
your life becomes genjokoan itself, see.
It manifests by itself as itself
as your life.

That's what Dogen Zenji talks about
at the beginning of the Genjokoan.
"When all Dharmas are Buddhadharma
there are Buddhas, sentient beings
delusion, enlightenment
life and death, practice.
When ten thousand dharmas are without self,
no life, no death
no Buddha, no beings
no delusion, no enlightenment."
What does he mean?
"Buddhadharma intrinsically transcends
these two aspects.
There are Buddhas, creatures
life, death
enlightenment, delusion."
What is he really talking about?

He says, "Furthermore,
even though it is so, flowers fall with our attachment;
weeds grow with our aversion."
What to do?
That's what genjokoan is.

How about your life—
all kinds of pain
all kinds of joy, happiness
and what?

Indeed it is an echoless valley.
How do you see that koan?
Isn't it a nice koan?
It's an interesting thing;
I talked about this koan before, see
and two people told me, "Roshi, I didn't understand
that very last part."
Indeed, echoless valley
seems to be very symbolic
most important part in a way,
best part of this koan that I am talking about.
I just talked about a bunch of them,
now that's the best part—
un-echoing valley, yourself, your life.
Why is it echoless?

Dogen Zenji said, I just read it—
because all self-contained,
don't need anything.
It's just like it says in the *Hannya Shingyo*:
No increase, no decrease
nothing is lacking, nothing is extra.
I understand that Sensei talked about *Bendowa*,
how to really practice,
how to go on the right way.
Sensei said in the first paragraph

what is the key there.
That's also marvelous writing too
I can make up a dozen koan
from that first paragraph right away.
Sensei said, *jijuyu-zanmai*
that's what it is, see
that self-fulfilled *samadhi*
that's what Dogen Zenji talks about.
That's what echoless valley is.
What to answer?
What is asked?
If you are called
sure, you respond
automatic.
Not responding
still it's a response.
Responding in an echoless way!

Maezumi Roshi in Salt Lake City, 1994.

Part Two
OTHER SELECTED TALKS

Mu

What is dharma?
Incomparably profound
and infinitely subtle,
it is rarely encountered.
For millions of aeons, see
it is hard to meet,
hard to encounter.
How come?
You see it, hear it
receive and maintain it.
What does that mean?

What we just chanted
is the *Gatha of Opening the Sutra*.
What is the sutra?
Sutra is the equivalent of the dharma.

You asked me to talk about koans.
That's what I have been doing.
Still I have one more day to sum it up
what koan is
and how to practice.

As a matter of fact
some of you are working on case koans
some of you, on Mu-ji.
But all of us in one way or another
are working on Mu-ji, see.

In a way you know the answer
and that is the problem.
One of you came to *dokusan*
complaining, Roshi, you are tricking us.
Mu-ji, what is Mu-ji?
There is no such thing!

If there was no such thing,
we wouldn't ask you to work on it.
What is Mu?
Is it some crazy stuff we deal with?
Can't be, is it?

A monk asks Joshu
whether a dog has buddha-nature or not.
Joshu said, No!
You shouldn't get too involved with yourself
but you should get more involved with the dog!
No? Why not?
Does a dog have buddha-nature or not?
What would you answer?
Ask Sensei next time to talk about this.
Mumonkan, the first case,
that's Joshu's dog, see.
And it's in the *Shoyoroku* too,

the *Book of Equanimity.*
The same koan, see,
but slightly different.

One time Joshu says, No.
Another time, Joshu says, Yes.
He doesn't always say, Mu mu mu!
We are not making any trouble for you,
but you are making trouble for yourself.
Mu-ji, what is it?
And if you say, I am Mu, No!
You're not Mu.
Are you?
Answer me!
See how bad you are!

What I am talking about
is the most meaty part of koan practice.
Am I right?

Dogen Zenji said all kinds of things, see.
Isn't it, I have to laugh.
Like this, fish and water
and bird and air.
"The bird is life and the fish is life.
Life is the bird and life is the fish.
Beyond these there are further implications and ramifications.
Now if a bird or a fish tries to reach
the limit of its element before moving in it,
this bird or this fish will not find it's way or its place.
Realizing this place, one's daily life is

the realization of the ultimate reality, genjokoan.
Realizing this way, one's daily life is
the realization of ultimate reality,
realization of koan."

What is this place and this way?
That's what Joshu is talking about, see,
this place and this way.
And when you understand that,
the realization of koan,
koan manifests by itself.
A nice passage.

"Since the place and the way
are neither large nor small,
neither subject nor object,
neither existing previously nor just arising now,
they therefore exist thus."
That's echoless, isn't it?
That's what Nangaku and the Sixth Patriarch talk about.
Who are you?
Who is that in front of me?
Where did you come from?
What is your life?
You can't say
it is big or small, this or that,
past, future
or even the present.
It's a famous koan, see,
the three times, past, present, future.
All together it's ungraspable.

If it's ungraspable,
how can you see that this is it?
I'm asking you!
What is Mu?
And definitely, Dogen Zenji doesn't say
it doesn't exist.
See, it just does exist.
What is that?
You can't even ask, see?
What else can you do?
What else should we do?
Best answer?
Shikantaza.

You do all kinds of side business;
that's what makes you confused.
You're supposed to do shikantaza
and you're not at all doing shikantaza,
but doing something else.
You come to tell me,
"I'm doing shikantaza,
I'm counting to ten, and working on koans."
In a way it makes sense,
and in a way, it's outrageous!
Indeed, you are inviting the problem yourself.
Yesterday Sensei told me
"I gave one talk here about Mu-ji.
And it was totally echoless!
They didn't understand what I said."
Yes, in a way it's a kind of understanding.

Mu-ji.

What is it, see?

There are so many instructions

about how to work on that koan.

All you should do is

just do it!

That is what you are told to do.

That's the easiest, surest way.

But you complain without doing it.

You just complain.

It doesn't work that way.

But if you just do it, it works.

That's how it has been practiced.

Now of course, everything has pros and cons.

That's why we have different ways to practice.

So I think Sensei is doing very nicely,

sometimes emphasizing case koans;

sometimes just letting you sit.

And in one way or another

your life is the echoless valley.

Regardless how you take it,

it is a complete thing.

Acting, reacting, responding, not responding.

Rising and falling.

All in itself it happens

echolessly.

Maybe an important thing to mention here is that

Buddha guarantees us,

our life is no exception,

the life of each of us is nothing but

the wisdom and compassion
of Tathagata Buddha's.
It doesn't matter whether you deny it or not.
Whether you accept it or not,
that's what it is, see?

Hakuin Zenji says in his famous *Song of Zazen*:
All beings are intrinsically buddhas.
He has an interesting analogy—
It is like water and ice.
Without water there is no ice.
And without sentient beings, no buddhas.
What's the difference there?
Ice and water.
Ice bangs into things, it's hard.
So, we should make it melt
if we want to be flexible.
So, how to make it melt?
That is to be our practice,
to actually experience that state of liquidity.
Not solidness.
Of course solidness is nice,
but better be flexible.
So, how to make it liquid?
Dogen Zenji says, "Forget the self."
Mu-ji,
the same, see?
Dissolve yourself into Mu-ji!
Don't hold on to yourself
when you are dealing with Mu.
Somebody told me,
"I put Mu in my stomach!"

It doesn't work that way,
you get stomachache.
Then sometimes it goes up to your head
and you become crazy!

So either way is okay—
let Mu-ji occupy yourself completely
or you give yourself away
all together to Mu-ji.
Either way it works.
But no half way.
It's the same with shikantaza.
If you really do shikantaza
you understand what Dogen Zenji is talking about.
But if there is a split,
you don't understand the absoluteness
completeness of your life, of your zazen
of your breathing, of your practice.
But when you really do it,
you appreciate.
Then the koan manifests as your life.

That is what Dogen Zenji says in the *Bendowa*.
Bendowa is a beautiful fascicle.
I want you to memorize all of it.
And take any passage as a koan.
Any passage is a beautiful koan.
Even in just the first sentence
I see dozens of koans.
Even each word.

"All buddhas and tathagatas
together transmitting *myoho*, subtle dharma."
For what?
In order to verify, confirm
anuttara-samyaksambodhi.
To confirm that
is the best way, unsurpassable way.
That's what shikantaza is.

But how come shikantaza is so good?
It is jijuyu-samadhi,
self-sustained, self-contained
self-fulfilled, self-fulfilling!
It's autonomous.
It all works by itself, see?
Jijuyu-zanmai, that's the key!
So working on Mu-ji
you can't be messed up with Mu.
But you are the one to take care of it,
whether it's Mu
or yes or no, yin and yang.
Doesn't matter, just take care of it.

It's an interesting thing, see,
Dogen Zenji says the main gate to get in that jijuyu-zanmai
"is tanza, straight sitting
and sanzen, penetrating Zen.
These two are the keys
to get into that main gate.
In a way he talks about zazen

as a means to get into that house
—whatever is inside, whomever is inside—
right through the front gate.

So we shouldn't stick too much to any particular idea,
then we freeze ourselves.
So we make ourselves to be quite flexible.
The really important thing is to confirm your life
as the *Hannya Shingyo* says
and as Dogen Zenji says—
no object, no subject
no this or that, no yin and yang.
And be rootless!
Don't stick to anyplace!
In one way or another, that's what we do.
No place to stick to,
then what's the problem?
That's in a way what Mu-ji is.
If you say, "This is it,"
you got stuck to it, see.
That's not it.

Then what would you say?
Anything? Everything?
Right there you got stuck.
Your very life itself,
nothing to do with it!
Isn't it?
What does your life have to do with all of this,
anything, everything?
So it shouldn't be ideas;
that's what Dogen Zenji talks about here.

Just exist as thus!

What's that?

In the *Diamond Sutra* it says "ungraspable."
Is it ungraspable?
Sure it's graspable.
Pinch your nose!
I'm not kidding.
Then how come it's ungraspable?
Grabbing it and yet not grabbing it.
What's that?
See, there is pain, joy,
and generally we believe
that something exists as me.
It doesn't matter if that's ego, survival,
consciousness or subconsciousness,
big or small,
deluded or enlightened.
We think something is here.
And what does the *Heart Sutra* say?
No gain, no loss,
nothing, no wisdom.
Not even no wisdom, that's funny.
There is not even no wisdom.
No wisdom, no gain,
that's what that means!

We say there is ego, there is no ego.
But we exist as thus,
as oneself.
And Avalokiteshvara Bodhisattva is the one

who sees oneself
who exists as oneself,
by itself, of itself, for itself.
It's very democratic!

I mention this because, being so,
you can be the Kanzeon Bosatsu!
Being so, you can really see what's going on
and what you can do.
I like that passage in the *Lotus Sutra*
where Kanzeon expounds the dharma to the buddhas.
He appears to the buddhas as a buddha.
To the shravaka and pratyekabuddhas
he appears as a shravaka and pratyekabuddha.
What does that mean?
To expound the dharma
Kanzeon goes through thirty-three transformations:
women, children, monks, laymen, laywomen,
even animals.
What does that mean?

It's a marvelous genjokoan!
All of you practicing,
really be Kanzeon.
Live the life of Kanzeon Bodhisattva.
What life could be better than that?

When you receive jukai,
what is that?
The most important part of jukai
is to realize your life as Mu!
That's what jukai means!

Of course, whether you realize it or not,
that's what it is.
No choice.
I'm not kidding.

How can anybody say the practice of Mu is fake?
If it is fake
we make it fake.
Actually it is not.
Your life can't be fake!

To receive jukai
is to take refuge in the Three Treasures,
Buddha, Dharma, and Sangha.
That's the most important thing.
What is Buddha Treasure?
Anuttara-samyaksambodhi.
What is that?
Rootless tree.
Supreme, unsurpassable,
the very best way!
Where no hindrance is found.
Nothing is held on to.

And what is Dharma Treasure?
Dogen Zenji simply defines it as
pure, clean and undefiled.
How do we make things defiled,
good, bad, right, wrong, clean, dirty?
Even to say *pure* and *genuine*
in a way is defilement too.
But we have to say something.

Genuine, apart from defilement, see
that's the dharma.
No yin and yang, no subject, object.
No separation.
If there is no separation
how can you compare anything
as if one thing is better or worse than the other?

This infinitely subtle dharma
is nothing but our life.
Even calling it pure and genuine,
that much is extra!
Such a genuine, solid, nice, unified thing
as our life
which exists as thus,
is the echoless valley
that Dogen Zenji talks about.

One lady asked the sisters
"The corpse is here,
where did the man go?"

What's left?
Buddha-nature is left.
Isn't it a nice way to say it?
If you don't believe it, I can't help it.
If buddha-nature is gone, what is left?
You're left as you are.
What's wrong with that?

I'm trying to put this together, see—

what case koan means,
what genjokoan means,
what our life means,
what taking jukai means.
And who is Kanzeon Bodhisattva?
What to do with your life?

All together, it's nothing but koan.
How to solve it?
In a way, such an attitude
is already a little bit out of place.
What is there to solve?
It's already solved.
And saying it's already solved
is not quite right either.
It has never been a problem!
I'm glad you laugh!

Many koans are like that.
"My mind is uneasy
it is not at peace.
Please pacify it."
Isn't that what you ask?
Bring me your uneasy mind!
There is no such mind!
"I am not liberated
please liberate me."
Who binds you?

Isn't it obvious?

This koan

"yes" "no."
Doesn't matter
whether it's yes or no.
What is buddha-nature?
That's what Dogen Zenji says:
instead of thinking about where is Mu or what is Mu,
consider what buddha-nature is.
That's what Bodhidharma says too.
To realize your own buddha-nature is
to receive jukai, to receive *kai*
to transmit kai.
Actually kai, that's what buddha-nature is.

What is the koan?
It's really nothing but MY life.
Not your life or their lives—
always MY life.
And when I really make my life
the life of the Three Treasures,
then everything becomes my life.
That's truly what buddha is.
Since we are baby buddhas
we try to grow up.
So all together,
in one way or another,
it's a wonderful genjokoan.
So please appreciate your life.

Kanzeon

In the *Maka Hannyaharamitsu*,
one of the fascicles of the *Shobogenzo*,
Dogen Zenji clarifies
what Kanzeon Bodhisattva is,
who he or she is,
and how he or she functions.
It is a "hundred grasses."
Hundred grasses means anything, everything.
And the very life of each of us
is no other than that.
And to really understand it
and realize it,
and live your life in such a way,
that's what *Maka Hannyaharamitsu* means.

Maka or *maha*.
You know what "maha" means.
We say *dai-ta-sho*.
Dai means big
and *Ta* means many.
And *Sho* means excellent.
In other words, quantitatively, qualitatively,
it's good, great, big.

That is maha, it has no outside.
That's big!
Do you agree?
Prajna is an interesting term.
According to the one who uses it
and the context in which it is used,
it could mean absolute wisdom,
and it could also mean a kind of knowledge
which is dualistic.

But when we say "maha prajna"
it always means absolute, transcendent.
That's how it can be translated,
but I don't like this word, "transcendent."
It's not transcendental or transcendent
but very, very realistic, see?
A real and matter of fact thing!
That's what Dogen Zenji says.
Anything, everything is prajna.
Hundred grasses
literally!
Concrete floor, see?
Lectern, paper, holder,
rug, ceiling,
you, your robe,
your hair, nose, tongue, body,
all kind of thoughts,
all kinds of so-called processes
of your mind or consciousness.
All these are nothing but that.
Maha prajna!

Then what is *paramita*?
All of you, again, know what it means, right?
"Reach to the other shore."
But not in the sense of sometime in the future.
You are already on that shore!
That's what "paramita" means.
You have gone already.
You have reached!
You have realized!
It's not in the past or present,
but in the perfect tense.
Have reached!

So, maha prajnaparamita means
that wisdom has revealed now as
not only just you
but as the life of anything, everything.
And we are living it!
And we are lived by it!
That's what maha prajnaparamita means.
And that's what Avalokiteshvara Bodhisattva does.

In *Hannya Shingyo* we read,
"Doing deep prajnaparamita. . ."
And Dogen Zenji says here in a beautiful way,
"Whole body's clear vision. . ."
this is not my translation.
"Whole body's" —*apostrophe* 's.'
Our whole body's clear vision!
What does that mean?
Whole body's clear vision, what's that?

And that apostrophe 's,' what does that mean?
How can the body have clear vision?
The whole body itself is no other than that vision!
Instead of being possessive,
we can take that apostrophe 's'
as an abbreviation.
The whole body is!
That kind of nondual vision
is what transcendent means.

Transcendent.
Not something to transcend,
but the life of each of us is transcendent.
That's the life we are living.
And when you really understand it,
then to understand what Mu is, won't be so hard,
and to live it won't be hard either.
You realize that there is
no other way that you can live.
It's not something
that you should try to do
tomorrow.

This prajna and one hundred grasses
are synonyms of Mu-ji, and definitely
Kannon Bodhisattva is too,
as well as dogs and cats
and ourselves.
However you are sitting,
I want you to really appreciate yourself
as Avalokiteshvara Bodhisattva.

You do shikantaza? It's fine.
It's koan? It's fine.
Whomever you are,
or whatever you do,
you can appreciate yourself as
Avalokiteshvara Bodhisattva.

Dogen Zenji says in the *Bendowa*,
even if one person sits
in shikantaza, zazen,
imprinting the buddha seal
upon body and mouth and mind,
then the whole sky, all of space
in other words, the whole universe,
becomes the buddha seal.

Anything, everything is a manifestation
of Mahavairochana Buddha.
That's what Mu-ji is!
That's what *dharmakaya* is.
That's why we chant,
"Pure Dharmakaya Vairochana Buddha."
We're not just mumbling the words.
It has clear cut implications!
Dharmakaya, that's Mu.

And Mu appears to be
the Mahavairochana Buddha.
And Mahavairochana Buddha appears to be
one hundred grasses,
and dogs and cats as well.

That's why Dogen Zenji says in the *Fascicle of Kannon*,
Avalokiteshvara Bodhisattva
is the Tathagata by the name of *Sho-Bo-Myo*,
Right Dharma Illumination.

And in fact, all of you
have Kanzeon's wisdom and compassion.
That's what we appreciate together
and make more and more illumined.
Illumined, not in a shiny, pompous way,
but illumined through our action!
The way we make a bow,
the way we do *gassho*,
the way we walk,
the way we serve.

Genjokoan

Dogen Zenji wrote the *Maka Hannyaharamitsu*
as the first chapter of *Shobogenzo*,
and then he wrote the Genjokoan.
But twenty years later,
just before he died,
he made Genjokoan the first chapter.
So you can see how much importance
he attached to it.

In a way, all Shobogenzo fascicles
are explanations of genjokoan.
Dogen Zenji talks about life as a genjokoan,
realization of the koan as your life
as the life of each of us
ordinary life or daily life or whatever we call it.
Without our life, no life exists as the genjokoan.
Seeing this is one thing.
How we live it
is the very focus of our practice,
the so-called acupuncture point.

Each fascicle of the whole Shobogenzo
is no other than genjokoan

and it all comes down to just one principle:
wholeness, whole activity,
full-functioning.
In other words, nondual life,
nondual activity,
which has no subject-object relationship
and no this or that.
No others and oneself.
Just all together as
one thing.

From this kind of perspective,
you can say, enlightenment and practice
are not two.
Can't be two.
Can't be separate, see?
The very life of each of us in any phase,
lying down, sitting, standing, working, walking,
it is nothing but expression—
the reality of life itself.
It is nothing but prajna wisdom
by which you see life as nondual
life as a whole
dharmakaya, dharma body, the dharma itself.
Dharma and yourself are not separate.
That is what transcendent wisdom is.
It can't be divided, see?

Of course, in a way we can divide it
but it is all together.
We should take it all together, as one.

No other way.
Regardless how fine senses you have,
if you perceive objects separate from yourself,
you can't function freely.
It's kind of a dead state.

Dogen Zenji talks about
the three dimensions of involvement
of life as a whole—
subject, object and perception
as one thing.
So these three parts are supporting each other
and because of that we can function.
It's not just me functioning;
and it's not objects
nor perception alone, either.

When you read the *Shobogenzo*
or other writings of Dogen Zenji,
you can apply this principle.
And basically, that's what I'm telling you, see?
You shouldn't see things in a dualistic way.

In other words, all of Dogen Zenji's works
should be appreciated as the genjokoan—
the koan which is the absolute, universal truth
which is your life.

So, what is it?
What is koan?
Koan is supposed to be universal.

Supposed to be a real public issue
which has authority for everybody, equally.
That's the koan!
The koan can't be personalized.
If you personalize it,
it's not koan anymore.
That's why it needs to be taken as a whole,
whatever we call it—
absolute, nondual, transcendent.
Transcending or going beyond what?
Going beyond the bondage of this "I"—
I, my, me.
My idea, my understanding, my belief,
which is a personal thing.
We call that *shan*, "my" something.
It's not koan
it's not public
not universal.

What is the quality of koan
that makes it public, universal?
No self. No I.
Isn't it clear?
I'm not saying it's easy to put yourself aside
but at least it's clear.
The koan can't be adjusted by personal bias.
If you do that, it's no longer a public document.
This is a very important point for those working on koans.
If you try to do it with your own something,
with artificial devices,
you are going the wrong way.

And regardless how much effort you put in,
you build up something that is not quite right.
It may even become harmful.

So when you work on koan,
the important thing is no I, my, me.
How can you do that?
Throw yourself into the koan.
Be the koan yourself.
So when we work on Mu-ji
become Mu yourself.
Either way it's okay—
give yourself altogether away to Mu,
or let Mu occupy yourself completely.
Nothing but Mu!
Give up yourself
and let Mu-ji take care of it.
In that way you can transcend the dichotomy.

Now of course, the "I"
is always most important, right?
But that "I" should be the same as Gautama's
when he attained realization and proclaimed,
"I and all beings
simultaneously attained the way"
—it wasn't just him.
Dogen Zenji says,
"It is hundred grasses and myriad forms."
Anything, everything, see, is no other than koan,
absolute existence,
dharmakaya.

Dharmakaya means "dharma body,"
not only as a human being
but as anything, everything.
To identify our being as dharma itself
is transcendent wisdom.
Dogen Zenji says:
When Avalokiteshvara Bodhisattva
practices profound transcendent wisdom,
it is the whole body's clear vision
that the five clusters are all empty.
Empty means wisdom!

These five clusters—
form, sensation, conception, discrimination, consciousness—
are five layers of wisdom, period!
Clear vision is wisdom, period!
Your body and mind!
Your eye, ear, nose, tongue, body,
your consciousness!
Isn't it clear?

The Four Noble Truths and prajna,
and the six paramitas, or ten paramitas,
and anuttara-samyaksambodhi—
when we objectively practice or study
the principles of this dharma,
it is very important to take these as your life.
Don't see all these teachings
as something outside yourself,
but make your life to be the dharma
or live your life as the dharma.

So not only the prajna paramita
but each one of the six or ten paramitas
is thorough, complete dharma
which totally occupies your life.
Your life is to be thoroughly identified
or confirmed, or clarified
by any one of these principles.
In other words, in such a way
you can make your life
practice your life
reveal your life
realize your life
manifest your life
as the dharma—
dharma itself, see?
Your life as the dharma body
which is no other than the Buddha's.
Because such life is the life in which the
anuttara-samyaksambodhi
the supreme, unsurpassable
perfect, best life is manifested.

Jijuyu-Zanmai

Jijuyu-zanmai,
self-fulfilling, self-sufficient samadhi,
is the condition in which we live.
It exists and functions naturally
and Kanzeon Bodhisattva represents that, see.
It doesn't matter, male or female.
Sometimes we say Kanjizai Bodhisattva,
Kan, to see or penetrate.
Ji, oneself.
Zai, is or to be.

To be and to function—
for me it's the same thing.
When we say, "to be," it's somewhat static,
not doing anything
but just existing.
We often take it that way.

Being and doing
may seem to be different
but they really are the same.
There is no such state as *just being*,
even for inanimate things.
See, here is a saucer,

but there is activity in it.
You know how matter exists.
Particles are in motion—
protons, electrons, neutrons—
and they hold things together.

They are active.
They are doing something.
It is energy.

Kanjizai is the one who sees
what the self is,
how it exists
and what it is doing.
It is the wisdom side of
Avalokiteshvara Bodhisattva.
Kanzeon is the compassion side.
This means realizing not only who you are
and what you are doing,
but also how other people are doing.

So how do we function together
in jijuyu-zanmai?
We are living in that samadhi to begin with.
All of us are Kanzeon Bodhisattva!
Then how do we appreciate ourselves
and how do we appreciate other people's lives?
Can we live together as the self-fulfilled samadhi?
Oneself is not limited to the individual,
we can also be One as a group.
One as a sangha.

Master Zuigan

Zuigan was the successor of Master Tozan,
the founder of the Soto school in China.
Tozan was a very meticulous person
and Zuigan had a little bit of that too.
He was always calling himself
"Hey boss! Are you in?"
And each time he was responding
"Yes, I am."
Can you do that?
"Hey boss! Where are you?"
"I'm someplace else!"
"I don't know," isn't it?

It's an amazing thing
always calling himself.
"Are you in?"
Answering himself
"Yes, I am."
And then comes the best part.
He would say
"Be awake! Be awake!"
And he would answer
"Yes. Yes."

Then next he would say
"Don't be deceived by others."
Isn't it nice?
Don't be deceived by others,
anybody, anytime.
That's a very severe statement.
Who are the others?
Can you tell me?
He's talking to himself, see
"Hey boss! Are you in?"
If you say "yes," is it really true?
Are you in?
Are you really there?
If you are uncertain,
you are deceiving yourself!

If you say "yes," that's fine.
But is it really true?
That's what he wanted to make sure.
Be awake.
Really be alert!
Be aware of what?

If you are aware of something else,
it's a joke,
it's a burden.
Isn't it?

So how to be really aware,
and of what?
Who is really the boss?

Of course, the answer is
Avalokiteshvara Bodhisattva.
That's the answer, see?
The Buddha!
That's the answer.
Is he really there
or is she really there?
And is she really awake,
you're not letting her sleep?
Maybe I should laugh.
I have been sleeping all day long.
Being in the zendo and sitting
and taking a nap,
and going down to the room
and lying down and taking a nap,
and during the night I am awake.
I don't know what I'm doing!
But anyway.

Be awake! Be awake!
And don't be deceived.
I love that part.
Don't be deceived by others
anytime.
Who are these others?
It's a wonderful koan.
In fact, my father loved this koan.
It was his favorite.
Don't be deceived by others.
That's the most powerful thing I learned from him.
Don't deceive yourself!

That's what it means.
No one deceives you
no one cheats you.
But you do!
And if you don't,
you are the Buddha, I guarantee.

So be alert, be awake!
Be Kanzeon Bodhisattva
and also let go.
Kanzeon can become anybody
in order to share the dharma.
He is a marvelous person.
The *Lotus Sutra* describes
thirty-three transformations of Kanzeon.
When he expounds the dharma to the buddhas,
he appears as a buddha.
To monks, he appears as a monk.
To laymen, he's a layman.
To children, a child.
Even when he expounds the dharma
to demons, birds, and reptiles
he appears like them.
What does that mean?
All of you are Kanzeon Bodhisattva
and expound the dharma as your life.
It is your life
it is your practice.
That is what you share.
Isn't it wonderful?
Be alert and be awake

and be Kanzeon Bodhisattva
to expound this marvelous dharma.
In one way or another
that's what we are all doing.
And don't deceive yourself
and don't be deceived by yourself.
Don't be deceived by the buddhas,
don't be deceived by Kanzeon Bodhisattva.

There is a nice poem that we chant
during the jukai ceremony.
"When sentient beings receive jukai
they merge with the buddhas,"
merge into the life of the Buddha.
In other words, when you receive jukai
you become the buddhas.
And all buddhas
become one with you
in accord with each individual.

Buddhas and sentient beings
well merged, unified.
No inside, no outside.
No division.
A perfect circle
complete.
Receiving jukai means
to confirm your life
as such life.
In other words,
confirm your life as the life of the buddhas,

the life of Kanzeon Bodhisattva.
Anybody has any objections?
If you do, raise them.
I will argue with you!
Your true nature is buddha-nature,
which is no nature.
No nature means no bondage.
You are totally free!
Liberated to begin with.
It's so true!

The Second Patriarch asked Bodhidharma
"My mind is uneasy
it is bound by something.
Please make it free."
And Bodhidharma said, "Who binds your mind?"
Who binds you?
This is always the universal
everlasting koan, see.
Sure, if you are not free, who ties you?
If your mind is bound,
who does that?
Nobody!

Nobody does that
including you!
And if you think so,
that's what Buddha calls delusion.
You are deluding yourself!

Shikantaza

Shikantaza means to just sit, isn't it?
That's what we should do.
If I can't, that's my problem.
When you really do it,
then right away, something happens.
But if we don't, nothing happens.

Shikantaza is just shikantaza
but we always add something extra.
And then it becomes something else.
It seems to me the key is this *shikan*,
just or wholeheartedly.
Just sit!
Literally, just sit.
That's the hardest part of shikantaza.
Simplest thing
and maybe the hardest thing.

Shikan is the most intimate way to exist,
that's what it really means.
It doesn't matter what you are doing—
shikan working, shikan sleeping,
shikan being sick.

Whatever you do
if you do it wholeheartedly,
it is perfect.
So just try to do it literally.
Just sit!

And not only physically,
let your mental activities sit too.
Simple as that.

It sounds easy
but I guarantee it is hard.
Like myself, I can't do it!
But it is a challenge, see,
to just really do it.
No questions are necessary;
the answer is always there.
Your question and answer
all together, it's self-contained.
The answer is just to be with yourself.
So the thing is, to really do that.
Then it happens.

That's what Dogen Zenji is trying to emphasize.
Shikantaza as the best way to appreciate
enlightened life.
It's an extremely simple formula
and it's the hardest thing to do,
because when you think about it,
right there is a big gap.

Being shikantaza, and thinking about something else
literally, there is a heaven and earth difference.
That's where the trouble starts.
Don't expect anything.
We don't need to,
there is nothing to gain.
What we want is right here!

Shikantaza is self-fulfilled samadhi.
It's samadhi, see, not thinking.
Things just as they are.
Just being
intimate with my life,
that's what it is supposed to be.
That intimacy is self-sufficient samadhi.
You yourself as you are!
And you do, as you do, as your life.
And I think that by sitting we understand and acquire,
perhaps most easily, that kind of state of being or doing.
That's why sitting is revealing.

Dogen Zenji never said that sitting by itself
is enough to realize what life is.
Straight sitting and penetrating Zen
is the right gate. That's what he says in the *Bendowa*.
Sitting is then almost like a means,
a scheme by which we get into the house.
Maybe there is a side gate or a back entrance,
but zazen is the front gate.
He doesn't say zazen is everything inside the house,

although in other contexts he talks about that;
in the light of shikantaza, it is everything
and not just the front gate.

In order to do shikantaza
it is crucial to have faith,
faith in the fact that shikantaza works.
Of course, you have to have faith in yourself too
and the fact that you can attain realization.
But what I want to emphasize here
is to simply have faith in shikantaza.
It is the best way to practice.
And when you really do it,
practice becomes realization itself,
and realization is nothing other than practice.

In the *Bendowa*, Dogen Zenji says,
"Since it is the realization of practice,
realization is endless.
And since it is the practice of realization,
practice has no beginning."

In other words, there is no time gap
between practice and realization,
but practice itself is nothing but realization, see?
And realization is nothing but practice.
So in each moment
your life manifests itself completely
as your practice, as your realization.
Which is so true, see?

The difficult part is that
we understand things in a certain way
and it is hard to drop our dualistic mind.
When we say practice is enlightenment
and the enlightened life is practice,
life is death and death is life,
it doesn't make sense, see.
Because we are not familiar with dealing
with the facts from a larger perspective,
we puzzle.
When we really try to understand with the body
instead of just with the head,
it's not difficult.

The True Dharma Eye

Shobogenzo, the title of Dogen Zenji's masterwork,
means "Treasury of The True Dharma Eye."
So, what kind of eye is that?
In the understanding of Harada Roshi
it can be divided into two, see,
the Right Eye and the Dharma Eye.
The Right Eye is the eye
by which you see the absolute side of reality,
the oneness or sameness.
And the Dharma Eye is the discriminating eye
by which you see the phenomenal world,
the world of difference.

When we only see the world of oneness
or only see the world of differences
we cause ourselves trouble.

I don't know about here in Poland
but in Holland, everybody wants to be equal.
It's a very free country.
In America, it's the same situation.
It is kind of nice, but it creates a problem.

Do you know why?
We ignore the fact we are all different.
But if we are only concerned about differences
it creates another problem.
We always end up comparing,
jealous of other people,
and we get upset.
Isn't it?

Even though we see the differences,
we may not really see them for what they are.
The same thing is true for equality.
Everyone talks about being one,
being nice and harmonious,
but do we really understand
what oneness means?

What is it that makes us all equal?
If you really saw that, there would be no problem.
So to have the Right Eye
and the Dharma Eye is important.
If we don't have both,
or rather, if we don't see in both ways,
we get into trouble.

Last night someone raised a question
about how to deal with fear.
I'm sure many of you have the same question.
The *Hannya Shingyo* gives a very clear answer.
See, even at the very first passage,
"Avalokiteshvara Bodhisattva doing deep prajna paramita,

clearly sees the five conditions are empty,"
then all suffering is eliminated.
And this suffering or pain
is very closely associated with fear.
We fear because we don't want to have pain.
Due to prajna wisdom
we are able to eliminate all fear.

So, how do we take care of fear?
Practice this prajna wisdom!
How?
See this emptiness.
Form is emptiness and emptiness is form.
When you look at life from the side of emptiness
that's the Right Eye.
When you look at life from the side of the five conditions
that's the Dharma Eye.
When you look at your life using both eyes
you see things in the proper perspective.
And when you really live with such vision
and put it into practice,
you will be Kanzeon Bodhisattva.

Kanzeon Bodhisattva is also known as
The One Who Gives No Fear.
What does that mean?
What is the opposite of fear?
What brings fearlessness?
Kanzeon practices deep prajna paramita.
When you do that, automatically something happens—
you see that the five *skandhas* are empty.

In other words, you understand who you are
and you see yourself as the one
who gives no fear, to yourself or to others!
And not only you give no fear,
but you become fearless.

So let me talk a bit about what koan is.
Ko means to make unevenness even.
Ko stands for the absolute part,
to make this uneven existence,
this world of differences, equal.
So how is that possible?
We see beautiful mountains and hills
and a beautiful valley,
how can you make this unevenness, even?
Mountains are high and valleys are low,
some trees are taller than others.
How can you make them even?
You don't need to!
They are what they are
and in that, they are equal.
That evenness, see, that is Ko.

Phenomena appear to be different
but they are both different and equal.
Mountains are high and valleys are low,
so to make them even,
we don't need to fill up the valleys
and flatten the mountains.
There is sameness involved
in the differences.

An means be as it is.
Mountain is high, as it is!
Valley is low, as it is!
That's An.
Man and woman as they are
young and old as they are
and being smart or dull, or strong and weak
pretty, ugly, however.
Just be as is!
In other words, this *Ko-An*
is a very interesting thing, see.
Ko stands for the absolute side
and yet it contains the relative.
An stands for the world of appearances—
everything as is, everybody as is.
All different! And yet,
it has the absolute as background.

Koan is a synonym for your life.
We study life! We penetrate life!
Using all the case koans as a mirror.
And without self,
reflect upon our life and see
the sameness and the differences.
When you do that, definitely
the koan will enlighten you.
That's what it means,
"To forget the self is to be enlightened
by ten thousand dharmas."
Anything, everything—

that's what ten thousand dharmas is.
That is to say, when you really forget yourself,
by anything, by everything,
you will be enlightened.
In other words, your life becomes
the life of everything!

Ju in jukai means to receive, to transmit,
to awaken to one's own nature.
Then we become the children of the Buddha.
So when we grow up
we become fine, grownup buddhas.
As babies, we don't really know what we are doing.
But one thing is for sure,
we are members of the buddha family.
So the significance of receiving jukai
is to make ourselves worthy enough
to be members of the buddha family.
And when you practice like you do,
I'm sure it will happen.

I have tried to clarify a little bit
what shikantaza is and what koan practice is
and how we have to practice.
What is the key point that we should be aware of?
Just sitting is not enough.
Definitely, just playing around with koans
is not enough!

Shikantaza is hard.
It is almost impossible.

So why not forget about it?
The thing is, you can't forget about it!
That's the problem.
That is to say, you're dealing with life.
If you can live life completely
and forget about it, it's fine.
But can you do that?
When the Buddha attained realization he said
that all of us have the wisdom and virtue
of the Tathagata Buddha.
We have his guarantee!
If so, how come we have to practice?
How come we are so stupid?
How come we have so much fear?
How come we are so uncertain about ourselves?
See, poor things!
That's our problem.

In a way, this dilemma is exactly
what koan is.
There is unevenness—
even the surface of our mind is uneven!
And there is evenness—
the absolute side which is reality,
which is the fact that I live!
My life is here!
This evenness or absolute side
and the unevenness side
constantly change
according to the environments.
They are constantly uneven!

What's wrong about having these two?
Evenness and unevenness
exist together.

Take it as is
and take life as is.
That itself is nothing but koan!
Emptiness is form, form is emptiness
itself is a koan.
And shikantaza,
that's the best solution, see?
Shikan, that's the key!
Just!
Just let it be.

And when you do something, just do it.
When you sit, just sit.
When you eat, just eat.
When you have fun, just have fun.
When you suffer, just suffer.
Then what's the problem?
Sure, if we suffer, there is a definite reason behind it.
Do you know what that reason is?
Emptiness!
—I shouldn't confuse you!
And because of that emptiness, you suffer.
And because of that emptiness, you have fun.
What's wrong with that?

Kai

Recently, a prominent teacher of the Soto School
said that *kai* is the natural self.
It's a very clear definition.
Kai is your buddha-nature.
We say *zen kai ichinyo*—
Zen and kai are one.
That is to say, when you understand what Zen is,
you understand what kai is, and vice versa.

We usually translate *kai* as "precepts,"
but that is not quite correct.
Of course kai implies the precepts,
but the deeper meaning of it
is not conveyed by the word *precept*.

In our tradition,
there are sixteen kai,
the Three Treasures, the Three Pure Precepts,
and the Ten Grave Precepts.
They are not sixteen different things
that we need to maintain separately,
but the kai are one thing

seen from sixteen different perspectives.
So in a sense, if you really maintain one precept,
you are maintaining all the others too.
What could that one thing be
that you should maintain?
It's your true nature,
your true self.
And what is that?
It is nothing but your life.
To receive jukai is to take care of that.
Going through the ceremony
doesn't mean that you get
something aside from yourself.
Receiving the kai is a confirmation or affirmation
of yourself, your life, as the Three Treasures.

So, to take refuge in the Three Treasures
means to reveal yourself, your life,
as the Treasure.
Bodhidharma said,
"To receive jukai is to transmit.
And to transmit, means to realize
your true nature."

Bodhidharma composed poems on all the Precepts.
About the Tenth, not speaking ill of the Three Treasures,
he wrote, "Self nature is inconceivably wondrous.
In the dharma of oneness, not raising the view
that buddhas and sentient beings are different,
that's what is called the Precept
of not speaking ill of the Three Treasures."
Isn't it nice?

That means, see
if your life is different from the life of the Buddha
you are violating that Precept.
Receiving jukai is a great commitment—
to live your life with such awareness!
You become a family member of the buddhas.
You become a baby buddha
and eventually grow up to be buddha.
Which is the truth!
Don't put another head on top of your own.
You remember that parable of Enyadatta?
It doesn't matter if it's a beautiful lady or an ugly man,
we all have our own head.
Ugly is fine, like mine.
How to really appreciate it?

About the First Precept, do not kill, Bodhidharma says,
"Self nature is such a marvelous thing.
In the everlasting dharma,
not raising the view of extinction,
that's what is called, *not killing*."
How do you really understand your life
as the everlasting life?
Sensei talked about the *Unborn*.
That means this unborn, undying life.
Don't raise the view of extinction of life, see?
Even if you really understand this one precept,
"Do not kill,"
you won't be afraid of anything.
And Dogen Zenji says about this
"Life is non-killing."
Not, "Life should not be taken," see

or, "shouldn't be killed."
It can't be killed!
That is a whole different perspective, see?
He says "Life is non-killing!"
In fact, the implication is
life cannot be killed!

Dogen Zenji said furthermore,
"The seed of Buddha grows continuously.
Maintain the life of Buddha's wisdom
and do not kill life."
That is what not killing means.
And to live such life
is the real significance of jukai.

Many of you have asked,
"How can we practice in everyday life?"
I think Sensei is very much aware
of how to take care of that.
He started to emphasize shikantaza
a couple of years ago,
which demands more awareness
of what's going on around you.
But still it may be hard to relate
practice to everyday life.

There is a koan,
"Ordinary mind is the Way."
I don't need to say much,
you work on that anyway.
Even when you don't work on the koan,
your daily life

has got to be The Way itself.
But between your true self and your apparent self,
there may be a gap.
And we can say that
to receive this kai, to have jukai,
is to fill up that gap!
After that,
how you take care of yourself,
that is to be your way
of maintaining the Precepts.

The Second Precept is,
"Do not tell a lie."
And Bodhidharma says,
"In the midst of the ungraspable dharma,
don't raise the thought of gaining
or grasping anything."
The dharma is ungraspable,
unknowable, inexplicable.
What kind of dharma is that?
Your life as a whole!
Mu
The Way.
And that way is ordinary mind,
your ordinary body and mind.
Don't tell a lie.
In the midst of inexplicable dharma,
what is lying?

Shakyamuni Buddha after attaining realization
taught for almost fifty years.
But just before he died, he said,

"I've never said a word!"
How do we understand that?
Life is inexplicable
because it has no limit!
It is infinite life,
limited as your life.
Limited, and yet limitless.
Talking, and yet not talking.
Living, and yet not living.
Unborn, and yet every moment being born.
Every minute dying, and yet it will never die.
We shouldn't limit our life
to what we think it is.
When you do that, you violate this wonderful kai.
Kai and Zen, it's the same.
When you understand kai,
you understand Zen.
And when you live kai,
you live Zen!

God

Do you believe in God?
That's a very interesting question, more than interesting,
it's a quite serious question.
When we as Buddhists are asked,
how do we answer?
It can happen to any of you, anytime.
How do you answer it?
Most of you were raised in the Judeo-Christian tradition
and people expect you to have some understanding
and maybe even faith or belief.

But for me too, if I'm asked that question,
how am I supposed to answer, see?
In fact, it happened twice very recently.
One time I answered that I definitely believe in God,
at another time I said, definitely I do not believe in God.
Why?
Because I always tell the truth!
I mean it.
Do you know what I mean?
Since the question is posed
from a relative perspective or sphere,
the answer is always yes and no.

And either way is true.
So I quite happily say yes one time
and I say no another time.
Nothing wrong with it.
Is it right or wrong?
Is anyone right or wrong?
That's my joke!

When we are asked whether God exists or not,
our belief makes a difference, of course.
Whether you answer yes or no
depends on your belief or understanding
of who God is.
But we understand everything
in a way as much as we understand,
and that isn't necessarily true understanding.
It rather openly invites arguments and questions.

What did Buddha say about this?
If Buddha was asked the same question
what would he answer, and why?
He himself was born in a rather high class
and his family followed the Hindu tradition.
They had of course the god Brahman.
Nobody denied his existence.
But do you know what kind of attitude Buddha took?
We can definitely learn from him.
He said, we don't really know what God is
and I will not spend any time trying
to know what is unknowable.
So he had a very pragmatic attitude.

Many people talk about God
and of course for those who believe
in the fact that God exists,
sure, God exists.
Why not?
But what about those who don't?
And we shouldn't mix things up.
Whether we have faith or belief in God or not
and whether God exists or not,
are two different things.

Some believe in God and some don't,
it's none of our business.
In a way yes, in a way no.
And if I do not know what God is,
if I don't have faith in God
as it is usually understood, that's fine too.
I can survive without having faith in God.
But it has nothing to do with whether God exists or not.
Personally, I'm quite happy and content
without having the blessings of God.
The Buddhas and Bodhisattvas are enough for me.

I'm sure, here in Salt Lake City
you encounter questions about God constantly,
since you're almost a neighbor of the Mormon Temple.
Everybody knows this is a very strong center of the LDS church.
And I want you to have very clear answers.
Not everyone of you needs to say the same thing—
then it sounds fishy!

You all have your own very distinct understanding
or appreciation of who or what God is,
and whether you believe in Him or not.

However you answer,
it's fine.
But you should have faith
in what you say!

Just don't say, "I am God,"
because it is not true!
Buddha never said that kind of thing.
How you phrase your answer is a very delicate matter.
With words you can so easily hurt other people
and that much you hurt yourself.
So be careful about that.

And even Buddha—
if you're asked by anybody
"Who is Buddha?"
how do you answer?
It's not easy, see.
And if you're asked further,
"What's the difference between Buddha and God?"
how do you answer?
If you grew up in the Judeo-Christian tradition,
you are supposed to believe in God.
Just one God!
So what is Buddha?
Buddha is not only Shakyamuni Buddha,
he is one of the transformations of Kannon Bodhisattva.

So I disagree if you say, "I am God,"
but if you say, "I am Kannon Bodhisattva,"
I will smile.

Whether or how you believe in God
is a very serious question for all of us.
Especially here for Kanzeon Sangha,
since you live so close to the Mormon temple.
How do we coexist with other religious groups?
—even on the same street!
So I think it's wise to be well prepared.
And if you have any excellent answers
before I leave,
please let me know!

Ceremony

I appreciate that you prefer
to sit in a more traditional form here.
It is an important part of our practice, see.
In our Center in Los Angeles
some are even sitting in short pants and underwear.
The fascinating part is
they don't seem to have any sense of
—I don't know how to say it—
respect for themselves!

And this is something I wanted to share with you.
Just before I went to Japan
I checked the word "ceremony"
and I found a very interesting thing.
The etymological implication of the word
is to heal, healing,
somewhat related to order,
order or form.
In other words, when we take care of things
in certain ceremonial, orderly way,
that in itself is a healing or mending
of some kind of disorder.
So that really hit me.

Americans like to take care of things
in a so-called informal way—
that means sort of loose.
But it easily gets disorderly.
If everybody starts doing things informally
and ignoring a kind of orderliness and unity,
what's going to happen?
It's a mess!

And unfortunately that actually happens
on an individual basis, in the family, and in society.
Freedom doesn't necessarily mean being casual.
Lack of formality can easily slip into lack of order—
physically, mentally, emotionally.
A sense of orderliness, formality, and unity
has a healing function—it's healthy.
When that is forgotten
we become disorderly, sick.
The physical body, the mind, and our emotions
are all together one thing.
When you get emotionally upset, you get physically sick
and vice versa.
So we don't need to think about formality
as something that is outside of ourselves.
It's not!
Ceremony means to do things orderly,
to take care of things in a healthy way.
It is a healing process itself.
If we arrange things together in a nice way,
there's a certain orderliness, a certain formality
and that in itself is healing.

In the zendo most of us wear the same robes.
We look the same and yet
each of us is distinctly different.
We're not like soldiers wearing the same uniforms
—not necessarily so.
We have a lot of freedom.
Being different and yet practicing as one
we function in a very healthy way.

The Four Dharma Seals

In the *Enmei Jukku Kannon Gyo*,
the sutra we chant every morning,
Four Dharma Seals are mentioned.
Sometimes they are called marks
but seal seems to me to be an interesting expression.
Special seal is still a little bit more descriptive,
a particular seal that gives authority to something.

We chant *Kanzeon Namu Butsu Yo Butsu*
U In Yo Butsu U En Bu Po So En
and then *Jo Raku Ga Jo*.
Jo, Raku, Ga and Jo are the Four Seals.

The first Jo means permanence, everlasting Jo
and Raku is comfort, enjoyment, happiness.
The third seal, Ga, means mine, I,
and the last Jo is pure, genuine.

We might think, why are these the Dharma Seals?
Usually the first one is called impermanence,
opposite of permanence, see?
And the second one, instead of happiness,

life is said to be suffering, pain.
The third seal Ga is self, I,
and instead of that we say "no I,"
no person.
Jo means genuine, pure.
How could that be?
Instead of life being genuine
we often say life is sinful, impure;
we're not doing something right and God condemns us.
Chases us to hell!

But anyway, all these Four Dharma Seals
are important aspects in life.
We should live in such a way—
with a sense of permanence
and delight in joy and happiness;
and make this Ga, or I, to be satisfied, comfortable,
content with this life.
Live life in a pure, genuine, clean and healthy way.

Jo Raku Ga Jo
in the *Enmei Jukku Kannon Gyo*
does not present the way
we usually think about life,
but rather how Kannon Bodhisattva understands
what permanence is,
and what real happiness and joy is,
and what this true "I" is,
and what is true, genuine and pure.
So this is a very important thing, see?

Then, how do we appreciate
these Four Dharma Seals in our lives?
That's what is also mentioned in the *Hannya Shingyo*,
another excellent sutra about Kannon Bodhisattva.
And I want you to really take it in such a way
that each of you is Kanzeon Bodhisattva.
That is to say that each of you must really understand
these Four Dharma Seals
which describe the most essential, valuable aspects of life.

In the Hannya Shingyo it says,
On Ri Is Sai Ten Do Mu So Ku Gyo Ne Han.
On Ri means being away, being apart from.
Is Sai means all, and Ten Do, upside-down,
and Mu So is deluded thoughts.
Mu literally means dream, dreamy thoughts.
Because of our upside-down dreamy thoughts
we think our life is permanent
and our pain
is something real that gets us.

On Ri Is Sai Ten Do Mu So
and then it says, *Ku Gyo Ne Han.*
When we turn away from all dreamy thoughts
all upside-down understanding
then we experience Ku Gyo Ne Han.
Ku Gyo means finally, and Ne Han is peace.

This self, this I, my, me, that we think exists
as the most important thing
is really fake!

When we accuse or blame someone, we may think
I am sincere, I am doing the right thing.
Even among us Buddhists it happens, no?
We make divisions between the different sects
and believe that ours is more genuine than the others.
Don't we do that?
It's all upside-down thinking,
daydreams.

What permanence is Kannon Bodhisattva talking about
and what kind of I?
What is real happiness?
What is it that gives us lasting peace?

In the meal gatha we chant
"May we exist like a lotus in muddy water,"
but also, *Shu Sei Kai Yo Koku*.
Shu Sei Kai means in order to live in the world
live Yo Koku, and Koku is empty space.

In the *Shobogenzo* there are three fascicles
about prajna wisdom.
Maka Hannyaharamitsu, *Kannon Bodhisattva*
and *Koku*, empty space.
Koku is like the vast, endlessly opened up sky,
that is the literal meaning of koku.
In other words, in order to live our life,
to live in society or in the world,
live like koku, like the vast sky!
And exist like a lotus flower

that grows in the midst of muddy water
and yet remains unstained.

Anyway, koku means empty
and to be at peace means to be like that—
your body and mind altogether
won't ever be disturbed, see,
just like the vast sky.
The sky doesn't mind what kind of clouds come up
what kind of winds blow
whether it is stormy or fine weather,
day after day, one after the other.
That's what it means to really transcend
attachment and detachment, pure and impure,
right and wrong, good and bad
you and me,
even enlightened and deluded
Buddhas and beings like us.
That's the real purity,
peace, nirvana.

We're so mixed up
evaluating and making judgments.
We think something is permanent
which actually is not,
and so we suffer.
Let's look at life and death.
After we die, what's going to happen?
That's a delusion for all of us.
Maybe you are still young and strong,

capable of doing everything you want.
Maybe you don't fear much
what's going to happen after death.
We live our life, but how do we take it—
do you really believe this life is impermanent?
If you think so,
you are still daydreaming.

Kannon Bodhisattva would not say this life is impermanent.
He says it is permanent, Jo, constant existence.
And that state is said to be the same.

Four years ago, I think I talked about this
in Amsterdam in some kind of church.
Or was it in London? Well, for me it's Amsterdam!
This is very important
it is the most fundamental thing—
in these Four Dharma Seals
we find the most unique characteristics of Buddha's teaching—
the first seal, impermanence or permanence,
Kannon Bodhisattva says that it is the same!

In Japan, when a priest dies
we don't use the word death, but *senge*.
Sen means to change places,
so to be dead means changing places to teach.
If you are Kannon Bodhisattva you really don't go anywhere.
You are always here!

It's fascinating.
In the *Lotus Sutra*, the Buddha says
—shall I read it for you?

I hope I can find it,
I am very well disorganized!—
"In order to save all creatures by tactful methods,
I reveal nirvana. Yet truly, I am not yet extinct
but forever here, preaching."
See, I am not making anything up!
What I say is based on the sutras.
Please don't think that I am just talking casually.
I'm not, see?

This aspect of Shakyamuni Buddha
we call the Eternal Buddha.
Kon Jitsu Jo Shikan
Kon means forever lasting
and Jitsu is actual.
Jo is the jo as in genjokoan,
it means manifesting.
In other words, Shakyamuni Buddha
is manifesting himself right here
and preaching no-death.

What's the difference between Kannon Bodhisattva
and the eternal Shakyamuni Buddha?
The Bodhisattva is said to be
the appearance of all buddhas.
That is to say, the life of Kannon Bodhisattva
is same as that of Shakyamuni Buddha.
And that is the life you live!
Permanent, everlasting life.

In one sense we appear in this world
and live 40, 50, 70 years and die.

We appear and disappear.
That's how we usually understand
permanence and impermanence.
But real life is not changing!
That's what Shakyamuni Buddha himself says.
"Just as an expedient means, I appear to be in nirvana
but actually, it is not so.
I am constantly, everlastingly here
to expound the Dharma!"
That's the real life!
And who is Shakyamuni Buddha?
This very mind!

So the true permanence is your life
right here now!

See how much we think in an upside-down way?
Do you agree or disagree?
When you practice prajna wisdom you turn away
from such upside-down, deluded, understanding of life
and stop daydreaming.
It makes you realize that
all buddhas in the past, present, future
attained anuttara-samyaksambodhi
and that all life is prajna wisdom.

Our views are upside-down.
We believe something that is not permanent
to be permanent,
and something that is permanent
to be impermanent.

By prajna, or absolute wisdom,
we can transcend all ideas of
permanence and impermanence.

So what is that transcendent state?
Not up in heaven.
Not anywhere else but here!
That's what the Buddha tells us.
Is it maybe hard to hear this?
If so, that much you are asleep
and dreaming.

So please go back to good zazen.
Practice deep prajna paramita
in order to verify, confirm, that your life is one
with that of Shakyamuni Buddha
and Kannon Bodhisattva.

GLOSSARY

The following abbreviations are used: Chin. for Chinese, Jap. for Japanese, and Skt. for Sanskrit.

anuttara-samyaksambodhi (Skt.) Supreme complete awakening.

arhat (Skt.) "Worthy one," one who has eliminated all defilements, the ideal of early Buddhism. Mahayana Buddhism considered this ideal as too limited and so replaced it with that of the Bodhisattva who vows to free all beings.

Avalokiteshvara See Kanzeon.

Baso Doitsu (709–788) One of the most outstanding Chinese Zen teachers, who had 139 successors; especially noted for innovative training methods that gave Zen a unique character.

Bendowa (Jap.) Literally, "A Talk on The Wholehearted Practice of the Way"; one of the primary texts on Zen practice, written by Dogen Zenji in 1231.

Bodhidharma (Jap., Daruma; 470–543?) Indian master who brought Zen to China where he became known as the First Patriarch; the twenty-eighth dharma descendent of Shakyamuni Buddha.

bodhisattva (Skt.; Jap. bosatsu) Literally, "enlightened being"; one who practices the Buddha way, but postpones entering nirvana until all beings have attained enlightenment; the ideal of Mahayana Buddhism.

bosatsu (Jap.) See, bodhisattva.

buddha (Skt.) Literally, "awakened one"; a term that variously indicates the historical Buddha, Shakyamuni; one who has attained buddhahood; and the essential truth or true nature of all beings. See also buddha-nature.

Buddhadharma (Skt.; Jap. buppo) The true realization of life; the way to attain that realization by following the teachings of Shakyamuni Buddha.

buddha-nature The intrinsic nature of all beings; true nature, true self.

Chosa Keishin (d. 865) Chinese Zen master, successor of Nansen Fugan.

Daito Kokushi (1282–1338) Japanese Zen master of the Rinzai school.

Denkoroku (Jap.) Literally, "Transmission of the Light"; the record of the great enlightenment of Shakyamuni Buddha and it's transmission by fifty-two patriarchs in India, China, and Japan.

Deshimaru Taisen (1914–1982) Japanese Zen master and successor of Kodo Sawaki Roshi, who went to France in 1967 and established a large international sangha.

dharma (Skt.) Universal law, reality; the teaching of Shakyamuni Buddha; manifestation of reality.

dharmakaya (Skt.; Jap. hosshin) Literally, "dharma body"; absolute reality beyond all discrimination; the unity of Buddha with all beings.

Diamond Sutra Or, "Sutra of the Diamond Cutter of Supreme Wisdom"; a core text of the Maha Prajnaparamita Sutra highly esteemed in Zen. It presents guidelines for bodhisattvas and sets forth the principle of emptiness.

Daito Kokushi (1282–1338) An honorific title for Myocho Shuho, Japanese Zen master of the Rinzai school.

dharma successor Title given to those who have received the seal of approval of their teacher. This seal is a certification of enlightenment and an empowerment to pass it on. See also ketchimyaku, patriarch.

Dogen Kigen (1200–1253) Great Japanese master who brought the tradition of the Soto school from China to Japan; author of the masterwork, Shobogenzo.

dokusan (Jap.) Literally, "go alone to a high one"; private meeting of student and Zen master.

Eihei Koroku (Jap.) Literally, "Universal Book of Eternal Peace"; collection of instructions given by Dogen Zenji and recorded by his students after the master's death.

Ejo See Nangaku Ejo.

emptiness (Skt., shunyata) Fundamental nature of all phenomena, which according to Buddhist teaching is unfixed and devoid of any everlasting substance.

Enmei Jukku Kannon Gyo (Jap.) An invocation of Kanzeon, chanted during ceremonies for the benefit of all beings and particularly for those in need.

Enyadatta (Skt.) A character in a story of the Lotus Sutra. Enyadatta thought she had lost her head and frantically looked for it. Her search is a metaphor for the search for enlightenment.

Four Noble Truths (1) Suffering, (2) the origin of suffering, (3) the cessation of suffering, and (4) the path that leads to liberation; the basic teaching of the Buddha.

gassho (Jap.) Literally, "palms of the hands placed together"; a gesture of respect and gratitude.

gatha (Skt., song) Short chant used in Buddhist ceremonies.

Gautama (Skt.) Siddhartha Gautama, the historical Buddha. See Shakyamuni.

genjokoan (Jap.) Literally, "The Way of Everyday Life"; fascicle of Dogen Zenji's Shobogenzo. The term genjokoan implies, what is manifest (genjo) is itself absolute reality (koan); all phenomena are the buddha way.

Gensha Shibi (835–908) Chinese Zen master, successor of Seppo Gison.

Hakuin Ekaku Zenji (1686–1769) One of the most influential Japanese masters of the Rinzai school, who systematized koan training and emphasized the importance of zazen.

Hannya Shingyo (Jap.) Literally, "Heart Sutra"; a short chant that expresses the heart or core of the Maha Prajnaparamita Sutra. See prajna.

Harada Roshi (1870–1961) One of the most important Zen masters of modern Japan; teacher of Yasutani Roshi, one of Maezumi Roshi's teachers.

Heart Sutra See Hannya Shingyo.

Hogen Bun'eki (885–958) Chinese Zen master in the lineage of Gensha Shibi.

Hyakujo Ekai (720–814) Great Chinese master who founded the monastic tradition of Zen and established rules of conduct for monks.

Indra Hindu god.

jijuyu-zanmai (Jap.) Literally, "joyful or self-fulfilling samadhi," the essence of Zen that has been transmitted from buddha to buddha down to the present day. See also samadhi.

Jizo Keijin (867/69–928) Chinese Zen master, teacher of Hogen Bun'eki.

jukai (Jap.) Literally, "receiving the precepts." The ceremony in which one formally becomes a Buddhist by receiving the precepts.

kai (Jap.) See precept.

Kanzeon (Jap., also Kannon or Kan Ji Sai Bosa; Skt., Avalokiteshvara) Literally, "the one who hears the cries of the world"; one of the principal bodhisattvas in the Zen Buddhist tradition, personifying great compassion and usually represented in the female form.

karma (Skt.) Literally, "deed"; universal law of cause and effect.

ketchimyaku (Jap.) Lineage chart of successive patriarchs from Shakyamuni Buddha down to the precept master and the jukai recipient. See also dharma successor, precept.

koan (Jap.) Literally, "public document"; recorded situation, event, or dialogue between a master and a student that expresses the teaching in a nutshell. Koans are used in Zen training as meditation devices. Nonrational in character, they cut through dualistic thinking and can bring the student to experience liberation.

Kodo Sawaki Roshi (1880–1965) One of the great Soto masters of modern Zen. He was the teacher of Uchiyama Roshi, who collected Kodo Sawaki Roshi's sayings in "The Zen Teaching of Homeless Kodo."

lineage See dharma successor, ketchimyaku.

Lotus Sutra One of the most important Mahayana Buddhist texts, recorded in written form about 200 C.E. In this sutra, the Buddha is not presented as a historical person but rather as a manifestation of the dharmakaya, which exists eternally. Every being participates in and can wake up to this transcendent nature.

Maha Prajnaparamita Sutra (Skt.) Literally, "Great Sutra of the Wisdom that Reaches the Other Shore"; a collection of about forty Mahayana sutras that deal with the realization of prajna and the functioning of the bodhisattva. The best known of these sutras are the Diamond Sutra and the Heart Sutra.

Maka Hannyaharamitsu (Jap.) Second fascicle of Dogen Zenji's Shobogenzo that deals with the Maha Prajnaparamita Heart Sutra (See Hannya Shingyo).

Mahavairochana Buddha See Vairochana Buddha.

Mahayana (Skt.) Literally, "Great Vehicle"; Buddhist tradition that holds the liberation of all beings as the highest ideal of practice and considers those who focus on individual enlightenment as followers of "Hinayana," literally, "Small Vehicle."

Manjushri (Skt.; Jap. Monju) Literally, "He who is Noble and Gentle"; the Bodhisattva of wisdom, often depicted riding a lion and holding a double-edged sword that kills delusion and gives life to wisdom. In Zen meditation halls, Manjushri is the principal figure on the altar.

meal gatha Chant used for formal meals in Zen practice.

Mu (Jap., or muji) Literally, "nothing, not, nothingness." When Joshu Jushin (778–897) was asked by a monk, "Does a dog have buddha-nature?," he answered, "Mu!" This dialogue is used as the opening koan in the Mumonkan and is often the first koan given to Zen students. The term "mu" can be used as a synonym for emptiness.

Mumonkan (Jap.) The Gateless Gate, a major collection of koans consisting of forty-eight cases compiled by the Chinese master Mumon Ekai (1183–1260). See also koan, Mu.

Nangaku Ejo (677–744) Early Chinese master; one of the two most important successors of the Sixth Patriarch, the other being Seigen Gyoshin.

nirvana (Skt.; Jap., nehan) Literally, "extinction"; it implies the freedom from the attachment to self; the blissful experience of absolute reality. In general, nirvana is used in contrast to samsara, the world of suffering. According to Mahayana Buddhism, nirvana and samsara are essentially one.

paramitas (Skt.) Literally, "gone to the other shore"; this term refers to the Six Perfections practiced by bodhisattvas as a gate to enlightenment and as an expression of their realization; the six paramitas are: giving (dana), morality (sila), patience (kshanti), effort (virya), meditation (dyhana), and wisdom (prajna).

patriarch A title used for all successors, male and female, who have formally received dharma transmission. The lineage extends from Shakyamuni Buddha through twenty-eight generations in India and six generations in China, down to Daikan Eno, the Sixth Patriarch. Since Daikan Eno, this transmission has not always been limited to just one successor and has branched out to different lineages up to the present day. See dharma successor.

prajna (Skt.; Jap. hannya) Enlightened wisdom; wisdom that transcends all duality.

pratyekabuddhas (Skt.) Literally, "Solitary Awakened Ones"; those who have attained enlightenment on their own and only for themselves. In their level of realization they are placed between arhats and buddhas.

precepts (Skt. sila; Jap. kai) Buddhist teachings regarding personal conduct that can be appreciated as ethical guidelines and also as natural expressions of one's realization. In Zen, there are sixteen precepts: the Three Treasures, to be one with the Buddha, Dharma and Sangha; the Three Pure Precepts, do not commit evil, do good, and do good for others; The Ten Grave Precepts, refrain from killing, stealing, greed, lying, ignorance, gossiping, elevating oneself and criticizing others, stinginess, anger, and speaking ill of the Three Treasures. See Jukai.

Rinzai Gigen (d. 866) One of the great masters of the T'ang dynasty in China and the founder of the Rinzai school of Zen, noted for its emphasis on realization and for the use of koans in zazen practice.

Ryutan Soshin Zen master of the ninth century; successor of Tenno Dogo.

samadhi (Skt.; Jap. zanmai) Literally, "establish, make firm"; meditative state of mind in which subject and object are not separated. See jijuyu-zanmai.

samsara (Skt.) Literally, "cycle of existences"; the realm of suffering caused by the illusion of a separate self; in Mahayana it refers to the phenomenal world and is considered to be essentially identical with nirvana.

sangha (Skt.) Literally, "crowd, host"; community of Buddhist monastics and laypersons; as one of the Three Treasures, sangha represents the harmony between the Buddha

Treasure and the Dharma Treasure; the realization and actualization of one's life.

Second Patriarch (Jap. Eka: 487–593) Successor of Bodhidharma, famous for his great determination to receive the teaching.

Seigen Gyoshin (660?–740) Chinese master who was one of the most important dharma successors of the Sixth Patriarch. See also Nangaku Ejo.

Sekito Kisen (700–790) Successor of Seigen Gyoshin and author of the poem Sandokai, literally "The Identity of Relative and Absolute," which is chanted during Zen services, particularly in the Soto school.

sensei (Jap.) Title meaning "teacher." In Zen, often used to refer to a dharma successor.

Seppo Gison (822–908) Chinese Zen master, successor of Tokusan.

sesshin (Jap.) Literally, "to collect the mind"; a Zen meditation retreat usually lasting seven days.

Shakyamuni (Skt.) Literally, "the sage of the Shakya clan"; this title is used to refer to Siddhartha Gautama, the historical Buddha, after his enlightenment.

shikantaza (Jap.) Literally, "just sitting"; meditation practice in which the mind is allowed to rest in a state of panoramic awareness without dwelling on anything in particular.

Shobogenzo (Jap.) Literally, "Treasury of the True Dharma Eye"; the masterwork of Dogen Zenji, generally considered to be one of the most subtle and profound writings in Buddhist literature.

Shoyoroku (Jap.) Literally, "Book of Serenity"; collection of a hundred koans compiled in the twelfth century by Wanshi Shogaku (1091–1157), a Chinese master of the Soto school.

shravaka (Skt.) Literally, "hearer"; originally a reference to the students of the historic Buddha or students in general; in Mahayana, the title refers to those who seek per-

sonal enlightenment and can attain this only by listening
to the teaching.

shunyata (Skt.) See emptiness.

Sixth Patriarch (Jap. Daikan Eno; 638–713) Great Chinese
  master often regarded as the father of Zen, who gave traditional Indian Buddhism a distinctive Chinese character.
  All the major lineages of Zen stem from the Sixth Patriarch.
  See dharma successor.

skandha (Skt.) Literally, "group, aggregate, heap"; term for the
  five components which together create the illusion of self:
  form, sensation, perception, discrimination, and awareness.

Song of Zazen (Jap. Zazen-wasan) Famous poem in praise of
  zazen composed by the Japanese Zen master, Hakuin
  Zenji (1689–1769). The Song of Zazen is often chanted in
  Zen services.

Soto One of the two most important schools of Zen in Japan,
  the other being the Rinzai school; founded by the
  Chinese masters Tozan Ryokai (807–869) and Sozen
  Honjaku (840–901). The name "Soto" is made up using
  the names of the two founders. The tradition of the Soto
  school was brought to Japan in the thirteenth century by
  Dogen Zenji.

sutra (Skt.) Literally, "thread"; discourses attributed to the Buddha.

Tao (Chin.) Literally, "way, path"; Zen adopted this word from
  Chinese Taoism and used it to indicate the Buddha Way,
  Buddhadharma, or the essence of Zen.

Tathagata (Skt.) Literally, "thus come, thusness"; the name
  Buddha used in referring to himself and which indicates the
  enlightened state.

teisho (Jap.) Literally, "recitation, offering, presentation"; a
  direct expression of a Zen master's realization, rather than a
  talk or lecture in the conventional sense.

Tenno Dogo (738/48–807) Chinese Zen master, dharma successor of Sekito Kisen.

Theravada (Pali) Literally, "teaching of the elders of the order"; the school that regards itself as closest to the original form of Buddhism; widespread in the countries of Southeast Asia.

Tokusan Senkan (781–867) Chinese Zen master of the T'ang period; teacher of Seppo Gison; dharma successor of Ryutan Soshin.

Tosotsu Juetsu (1044–1091) Chinese Zen master of the Rinzai lineage.

Tozan Ryokai (807–869) Chinese Zen master. See Soto.

Three Treasures See Buddha, dharma, sangha.

Vairochana Buddha (Skt.) Literally, "He Who is Like the Sun"; one of the five transcendent Buddhas, often depicted with his hands in the gesture of supreme wisdom.

Way (or The Way) See Tao.

yin and yang (Chin.) In Taoist philosophy, the two polar energies; the source of the universe; yin refers to the feminine, receptive aspect, and yang to the masculine, active aspect.

zazen (Jap.) Literally, za means "sitting" and zen, "meditation"; the practice of Zen meditation. Although the root of the word "zazen" lies in the Sanskrit dhyana, meaning meditative absorption or concentration, zazen does not truly refer to these practices. The word has been used over time to indicate jijuyu-samadhi. See Zen.

Zen (Jap.; Chin., ch'an; Skt., dhyana) An abbreviation of zazen; the school of Buddhism that emphasizes the practice of zazen.

zendo (Jap.) Zen meditation hall.

zenji (Jap.) Literally, "Zen master"; an honorific title used for a great or renowned Zen master.

Zuigan Shigen (Jap.) A ninth century Chinese master.

CALLIGRAPHIES AND PHOTOS

Calligraphies by Maezumi Roshi. Photos by Sangha members.

ACKNOWLEDGMENTS

There are many people that I would like to thank for making this publication possible. In fact, I feel indebted to the whole Kanzeon Sangha who created the context for the book. Those whom I would like to thank personally are first of all, Genpo Merzel Roshi, who has been my teacher for twenty years now and my direct link to Maezumi Roshi; and Daido Loori Roshi for his encouragement and for publishing a part of the manuscript through Dharma Communications. Regarding the actual work of transcribing and editing, I am most grateful to Wynn Seishin Wright, who assisted me for long hours throughout the process. Furthermore, I want to thank Stephen Muho Proskauer for his help and wise advice, Alexa Shodo Postema for getting me started on the project, and my wife, Tamara Myoho Gabrysch for her support and patience.

—Anton Tenkei Coppens